D1428729

David Nylund

Foreword by Gene Combs, M.D.

Treating Huckleberry Finn

To my son Drake and all other children who embrace nonconformity

Treating
Huckleberry
Finn

A New Narrative Approach to Working with Kids Diagnosed ADD/ADHD

JOSSEY-BASS
A Wiley Company
www.josseybass.com

Published by

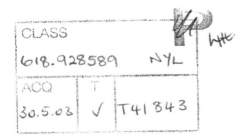

JOSSEY-BASS
A Wiley Company
989 Market Street
San Francisco, CA 94103-1741

www.josseybass.com

Copyright © 2000 by John Wiley & Sons, Inc.

FIRST PAPERBACK EDITION PUBLISHED IN 2002

Jossey-Bass is a registered trademark of John Wiley & Sons, Inc.

Jossey-Bass books and products are available through most bookstores. To contact Jossey-Bass directly, call (888) 378-2537, fax to (800) 605-2665, or visit our website at www.josseybass.com.

Substantial discounts on bulk quantities of Jossey-Bass books are available to corporations, professional associations, and other organizations. For details and discount information, contact the special sales department at Jossey-Bass.

We at Jossey-Bass strive to use the most environmentally sensitive paper stocks available to us. Our publications are printed on acid-free recycled stock whenever possible, and our paper always meets or exceeds minimum GPO and EPA requirements.

Library of Congress Cataloging-in-Publication Data

Nylund, David.
  Treating Huckleberry Finn : a new narrative approach to working with kids diagnosed ADD/ADHD / David Nylund.—1st ed.
      p. cm.
Includes bibliographical references and index.
  ISBN 0–7879–5229–X (alk. paper)
  ISBN 0–7879–6120–5 (paper)
  1. Attention-deficit hyperactivity disorder. I. Title.
RJ506.H9 N954 2000
618.92'8589—dc21   00–008176

FIRST EDITION
HB Printing   10 9 8 7 6 5 4 3 2 1
PB Printing   10 9 8 7 6 5 4 3 2 1

Contents

Foreword

Maybe I have ADHD. When I read Huck Finn's words about school (". . . it was deadly dull, and I was fidgety"), I was reminded of many dull hours I spent fidgeting at my desk. I always got "talks and disturbs others" checked on my report card. I got at least one "you're not living up to your potential; you should be working harder" speech from the principal each semester of grade school and high school. Fortunately, I finished all that long before what David Nylund calls the pandemic of ADHD swept through our nation.

Huck Finn and I go way back. I first made his acquaintance in the fourth grade. Being raised in hillbilly country, where people didn't talk like television announcers, I was filled with excitement to find a book with a central character who talked like my friends. Up to that point, I thought everybody in books talked like city folks. Finding Huck was incredibly freeing and inspiring—so much so that on my next one-page writing assignment in school, I wrote with my best approximation of Huck's spelling and grammar!

Imagine the effect it had on me when my teacher responded by hand-delivering the piece to my desk, where she then gave me a loud and long dressing down for being insubordinate and disrespectful. Up to that moment, I had been feeling happy. I was proud of what I had written and thought she would be, too. After all, she was the person who suggested I read Huckleberry Finn in the first place. From that moment on, I mistrusted my abilities as a writer. I was also wary about the trustworthiness of people in positions of power over me. It took me many years to find a sense of excitement and confidence about writing again. And this was just from one incident! If I had actually been labeled as having a disease like Attention Deficit Hyperactivity Disorder, and if, instead of just my fourth grade teacher, many experts had reinforced that label, I probably wouldn't be writing this Foreword. I'm truly glad to have escaped the pandemic.

In this book, David Nylund raises and addresses some very important questions about how parents, teachers, physicians, and therapists should relate to children. These questions concern values and aesthetics, and they extend well beyond the specific problem of ADHD: Do we want our schools to focus on predictability, turning out a uniform product, or do we want children to be imbued with a sense of wonder and a valuing of originality? Do we want the model of adult-child interactions to be that of experts treating passive bodies with one-size-fits-all prescriptions or that of human beings with different kinds of knowledge collaborating to find tailor-made ways to address particular problems? Do we want children to grow up with unquestioning obedience or with courage and cultural resistance?

Nylund begins the book with a clear, well-reasoned, and well-researched critique of the so-called science that is used to support the validity of ADHD. As a psychiatrist, I am often embarrassed by the current standard practices of my profession. Biologic reductionism, masquerading as "hard science," seems to have hypnotized an overwhelming number of my psychiatric colleagues. It has taken control of all the major journals. The kind of studies that Nylund debunks in the first part of this book fill their pages. And between the articles are glossy, full-color ads that would make any snake oil salesman proud. The ads hawk psychotropic drugs.

Another current practice of my psychiatric colleagues that I find embarrassing is the use of checklists to replace curious conversation. Nylund shows how this practice can have deleterious effects for children who find school deadly dull, as well as for their teachers, parents, and therapists. This book is full of suggestions and illustrations of how we might, instead, work to privilege the child and family's unique sociocultural situation and their own understanding of their concerns.

Because managed care is so frequently blamed for supporting, if not causing, the rush to judgment that characterizes almost all doctor-patient (and therapist-client) interactions these days, it makes a difference that David Nylund has worked for many years on the front lines of a large managed care organization. He speaks with the voice of experience. The attitudes, values, and practices that he describes in this book are effective in a managed care setting. He clearly and interestingly illustrates how "counter instruments" such as "the SMART scale" and "the environmental checklist" can be used to patiently, collaboratively, and respectfully unpack family members' understandings of ADHD.

To me, one of the most admirable things about the book you are about to read is that it describes many effective acts of resistance to harmful cultural trends without ever being small-minded or over-reactive. Nylund is clear about why he advocates the ideas and practices he sets forth here without pathologizing people who hold other views. I found his suggestions for how to work with people who are heavily invested in the diagnosis of ADHD to be clear, even-handed, and above all, useful. His stance in relation to medication is also balanced and reasonable.

The bulk of the book describes the SMART approach to working with ADHD. This postmodern approach, closely related to the narrative therapy of White and Epston, is divided into five steps, and each step is clearly modeled in a separate chapter. Nylund gives plenty of examples and orients readers to each step in a way that is clear without being prescriptive. The penultimate chapter on the SMART classroom should be read by all parents and teachers.

I doubt that Huck would read this book. He'd rather "light out for the Territory ahead of the rest." But I'm sure that if he met David Nylund along the way, he'd be glad to have him as a traveling companion.

This book is proof that David has been exploring the Territory, so I know he's out there. I'd like to listen in when he and Huck meet up.

Evanston Family Therapy Center   Gene Combs, M.D.
Evanston, Illinois   *March 2000*

Preface

One night not long ago, my five-year-old son Drake chose *The Adventures of Huckleberry Finn* for his bedtime story. We dove into Huck's world of imagination, courage, and mischief. As a father I was warmed by my son's enthusiasm for the story. As a reader I was captured by Huck's spirit and sense of adventure. But as a clinician I couldn't help but wonder: If Huck were alive today, would his rebellion and individualism be perceived as more than just problematic behavior? As the story unfolded I was troubled by the thought that if he were living today, Huck Finn would probably be diagnosed as having ADHD (attention deficit hyperactivity disorder). He would probably be taking Ritalin.

After all the adventure in his bedtime story, putting Drake to bed was a challenge. "No!" he said. "I don't want to go to sleep yet." He fidgeted and played, crafting one ploy after another to delay his bedtime. Like Huck—maybe even inspired by Huck—he turned the evening into an adventure complete with treasure hunts, tall tales, and great escapes. I was both frustrated and amused.

When Drake finally drifted off to sleep, I fell into my own preoccupations: where I needed to be the next day and how I would get a sleepy child up and ready for school on time. But at the same time, I realized my kinship with Huck's fictional guardians, the Widow Douglas and Miss Watson. We are bound by the experience of trying to parent a spirited child. It is difficult, even today, to include such a child's preferences and interests in daily life and to avoid ruling the child with fear. When I used to imagine the kind of father I wanted to be, I knew I didn't want to use fear as discipline—to tame my son's desires by making him worried or scared. I wanted to find a way to parent him that would enliven his voice and empower him to make choices—to treasure his courage, compassion, and emerging Huck-like spirit.

But Drake is now in kindergarten. I am worried about whether the qualities I value in him will be appreciated in his new classroom. What if he fidgets too much? Will he resist following the rules? Will he act up? (He certainly does at home.) At another time in history, these behaviors may have been considered normal, even if they were troublesome. But in today's classrooms, they could make my son vulnerable to a diagnosis of ADHD—a psychiatric disorder. Each year tens of thousands of children are given such a diagnosis, with devastating consequences for their minds, bodies, families, futures, and lives.

The Marketing of ADHD-Ritalin

My work with children and families in a large HMO (health maintenance organization) lets me see, on a daily basis, the effects of ADHD on parents, teachers, therapists, social workers, and psychiatrists. ADHD is marketed to all of us as a biological disorder that causes children (and some adults) to exhibit a range of problematic behaviors: distractibility, hyperactivity, and difficulty listening, paying attention, and following directions; fidgeting is also part of the syndrome.

According to Novartis (formerly Ciba-Geigy), a large manufacturer of pharmaceuticals, the best "treatment" for this "disorder" is the prescription amphetamine, Ritalin. Although it is a stimulant, Ritalin is alleged to improve attention and reduce hyperactivity in "ADHD children." The company also markets to therapists, parents, and teachers an expensive series of books, videotapes, support groups, and classes to help them "manage" their "difficult children." If Huck were alive today, his teachers and care providers would, without a doubt, find themselves tempted by the promises of ADHD and Ritalin.

Understandably, many parents, teachers, and therapists who are constantly confronted with serious behavior problems and limited resources have responded with enthusiasm to the idea that ADHD is a biological disorder with a medical treatment. So much excitement has been generated that sales of Ritalin have grown by 700 percent since 1990, making it one of the most frequently prescribed medications in the United States. And *ADHD* has become a household term. Like a steamroller, the ADHD-Ritalin machine forces its way through our families, schools, and clinics, flattening everything in its path. This leaves me with grave concerns for my son and for millions of other children. If Huck Finn were alive today, what would his teachers, clinicians, and care providers say about him? Would there be room for his rebellion? His courage? His imagination? Or would he be viewed only through the lens of compliance and obedience, found lacking, and subjected to chemical restraint? Would the world be denied a hero?

Although losing Huck Finn to Ritalin would have been tragic for literature, my own concerns are more personal and direct. Will a teacher in Drake's future view his spirit as an obstacle in the classroom? Will he be subjected to an ADHD assessment? Will a psychiatrist tell me he needs medication? If I have a different perspective from his teacher or therapist or psychiatrist, will I be seen as a neglectful or noncompliant parent? Or will I be accused of letting my child be "in charge" of me? Will the choices in my life be subjected to scrutiny while well-intentioned teachers, therapists, and physicians pick my life and my values and my child apart? How will I respond? My guess is that if those things happen, my response will be similar to the responses of hundreds of parents with whom I've worked. I'll feel varying degrees of relief, anger, guilt, shame, embarrassment, resentment, and hope.

As a mental health practitioner, I am keenly aware of the seductive nature of the ADHD label for parents and professionals.

The problems that children exhibit can be overwhelming. Community resources to solve these problems are diminishing; ADHD and Ritalin seem to promise a quick, easy answer to a challenging dilemma.

Audience for This Book

If you are worried, as I am, about the high cost of using ADHD-Ritalin as an easy way out of dealing with hard problems, this book is for you. Perhaps you are trying to parent a spirited child. Or you may be one of the growing numbers of mental health professionals concerned about what the ADHD-Ritalin juggernaut is doing to our children. Or you may want to learn specific, alternative ways of working with children who have been described as ADHD. If so, this book is for you.

Or perhaps you are a teacher who is looking for fresh ideas to engage children who are influenced by inattention, hyperactivity, or temper. Or you may be concerned that children's spirits are being constrained by medication. Or you might like to *raise* your Huck-like children rather than *restrain* them. If any one of these descriptions fits you, you should find this book helpful, challenging, and stimulating to your work. I intend to take you on an adventure much like Huck's on the Mississippi River so many years ago. We will stand up to conventional thinking. We will rely on our ingenuity and our courage. We will let our conscience and our curiosity guide us.

Contents of the Book

I begin my challenge to the prevailing opinion about ADHD-Ritalin by showing what's wrong with it.

Criticism of the ADHD-Ritalin Approach

First of all, the ADHD-Ritalin marketing campaign withholds important information about the ADHD diagnosis and its effects on children and their families. Here is some of what is left out:

- There is little evidence that ADHD exists as a discrete biological phenomenon.
- The ADHD diagnostic process is highly subjective.
- Ritalin causes serious, lifelong side effects for many users.
- There is no evidence that Ritalin solves the complex behavior problems that are attributed to ADHD.
- The pharmaceutical companies, schools, and other mental health care industries that promote the disorder make substantial profits by doing so.

The ADHD-Ritalin marketing effort has also failed to answer these basic questions:

Does ADHD really exist?

Would other social conditions or influences better account for children's behavior problems?

Does Ritalin actually solve the problems its manufacturer says it will solve?

Are there other, better ways to solve those problems?

In the first part of the book, I show that ADHD is not a discrete medical condition but a *social construct*—a way of explaining certain behaviors or phenomena that is derived from our current social environment and from the public discourse about children, families, and schools. And we'll see that viewing ADHD as a construct leads to interesting questions:

Whose interests are being served by the idea that ADHD is a biological condition? Whose interests are subjugated?

Why is ADHD so popular at this time in our history?

What effects does medicalizing this problem have on children, families, professionals, and society?

I reveal what's behind the ADHD epidemic and argue that diagnosing children with ADHD has a stigmatizing and disempowering effect on them. Issues to be explored include

- How cultural factors, the ADHD industry, biological psychiatry, and the Western school system have made ADHD so pandemic
- The limitations and subjective nature of the diagnostic process
- The contradictions and gaps in the biological research on ADHD
- The devastating effects of labeling children ADHD
- The potential harmful effects of Ritalin and other stimulant medication
- A discussion of who tends to be most vulnerable to being labeled
- A critique of our current educational system

Alternatives to ADHD-Ritalin: The SMART Approach

You may find yourself thinking, "OK, but how *do* I work with problems such as hyperactivity, distractibility, and aggression?" This is an important question. These problems are distressing and sometimes devastating to children and families. They are also serious problems for therapists to confront. The intention of this book is not to minimize or mask the severity of the behavior problems that parents, teachers, children, and clinicians face. Rather, the intention is to reveal the pretense of the ADHD diagnosis and make room for creative, useful strategies to improve children's behavior.

In the second part of the book, I show how therapy can address problems associated with ADHD. I offer a step-by-step guide to working with ADHD children that I call the SMART approach. This approach helps children harness their abilities, knowledge, and talents. The five steps of the SMART approach are

Separating the problem of ADHD from the child

Mapping the influence of ADHD on the child and family

Attending to exceptions to the ADHD story

Reclaiming special abilities of children diagnosed with ADHD

Telling and celebrating the new story

Subsequent chapters offer ways to work collaboratively with parents, professionals, and schools, along with innovative ideas to highlight children's competencies. Included are

- Assessment tools that highlight children's strengths instead of their deficits
- Creative teaching methods that engage children who struggle with inattention and learning problems
- Strategies that parents can use at home to empower children diagnosed with ADHD

I hope that *Treating Huckleberry Finn* will inspire you—that it will help you see therapeutic possibilities that you could not see through the lens of the traditional ADHD-scope. Ultimately, I hope that reading this book will get you to think twice before labeling a child ADHD. My son Drake and many other children with the courage and imagination of Huck Finn will be better off when we stop pathologizing children of difference.

Acknowledgments

I wish to acknowledge Alan Rinzler, my Jossey-Bass editor, for his encouragement in writing this book. His support, experience, and guidance were of immeasurable value.

I am forever grateful to my wife, Debora, for her significant contributions to this book. First, I am indebted to her for believing in me and for her ongoing feedback about the manuscript and unending support and patience as the book developed. Her love, assistance, and wisdom inspired and nurtured me throughout the project.

I extend a special note of appreciation to Rob Brownell for his graphics assistance, to Roberta Medina for her word processing skills, and to Irene Borrego, Tracy Candini, Linda Metcalf, and Scott Clary for their contributions to Chapter Ten.

I appreciate all my colleagues at Kaiser and La Familia for sharing their ideas and skills with me, the students with whom I have the privilege of supervising, and the clients who continue to teach me.

I want to thank the following people who have significantly shaped my thinking: Harlene Anderson, Peter Breggin, Jeff Chang, Jennifer Freeman, Jill Freedman, Victor Corsiglia, Lynn Cooper, David Demetral, Vicki Dickerson, David Epston, Paulo Freire, Howard Gardner, Gene Combs, Melissa Griffith, James Griffith, bell hooks, Michael Hoyt, Ian Law, Bill Lax, Dean Lobovits, Stephen Madigan, Scott Miller, Toni Morrison, Bill O'Hanlon, Thich Nhat Hahn, Colin Sanders, Craig Smith, John Thomas, Karl Tomm, Kathy Weingarten, Michael White, and Jeffrey Zimmerman. Your ideas have been a source of inspiration and generativity to me. Your collective voices are in this book.

Sacramento, California   David Nylund
May 2000

Treating Huckleberry Finn

If a man does not
keep pace
with his companions,
perhaps it is because he
hears a different drummer.
Let him step to the
music which he hears,
however measured or far away.

—Henry David Thoreau

Part One

The Critique

Chapter One

Introduction

Huck Finn Meets Dr. Chad Geigy

The Widow Douglas, she took me for a son, and
allowed she would sivilize me; but it was rough
living in the house all the time, considering how
dismal regular and decent the widow was in all her
ways; and so when I couldn't stand it no longer, I
lit out. . . . Her sister, Miss Watson, a tolerable slim
old maid, with goggles on, had just come to live
with her, and took a set at me now, with a spelling
book. She worked me middling hard for about an
hour, and then the widow made her ease up. I
couldn't stand it much longer. Then for an hour it
was deadly dull, and I was fidgety.

—*Huckleberry Finn in* The Adventures of Huckleberry Finn,
Mark Twain

But I've wondered: Is there a place for childhood in
the anxious downsizing America of the late 1990s?
What if Tom Sawyer or Huckleberry Finn were to
walk into my office tomorrow? Tom's indifference
to schooling and Huck's "oppositional" behavior
would surely have been cause for concern. Would I
prescribe Ritalin for them too?

—*Lawrence Diller, M.D.*

What if Huckleberry Finn were alive today, living in some sub-
urban community with all his oppositionality, nonconformity, and

indifference to schooling? Would he be in serious trouble at home and in school? Would he find himself referred to a psychiatrist for an evaluation? Would he be diagnosed with attention deficit hyperactivity disorder (ADHD), and would his physician prescribe Ritalin?

In Mark Twain's novel, Huck Finn is being watched over by the Widow Douglas and her sister, Miss Watson. They attempt to civilize him by dressing him in nice clothes, forcing him to attend school, and trying to teach him the basics of reading, writing, and math. For the most part, he doesn't like that. Huck particularly rebels against the strict ways of Miss Watson, who attempts to force religion on him and makes him quit smoking.

One evening Huck sneaks out for a smoke and meets up with his friend in mischief, Tom Sawyer. When he returns home later that night, the Widow Douglas scolds and lectures him about religion, which he doesn't appreciate at all.

Suppose at this point in the story, the Widow Douglas is, in fact, Huck's foster parent, and the year is 2000. What might happen next?

An Imaginary Scenario

Given Huck's recurrent behavior problems and negative comments from teachers and other parents, the Widow Douglas might very well decide to take Huck to a mental health practitioner. Let's say she chooses Dr. Chad Geigy, a child psychiatrist at a local HMO. She has recently read about attention deficit disorder and wonders if that's the cause of Huck's rebellion. So after she and Huck's teacher have filled out a Connors Rating Scale for ADHD, she takes the boy in for a first session, and the following interview ensues:

> *Dr. Geigy:* Welcome! Come on into my office. [Huck looks around the room and eventually sits down. It's clear from his annoyed expression that he doesn't want to be there. While

Dr. Geigy starts the interview, Huck fidgets, looks out the window, and appears restless.] Hi, I'm Dr. Geigy. What's your name?

Huck: Huck.

Dr. Geigy: Hi Huck. How old are you?

Huck: I'm twelve.

Dr. Geigy: I see. I understand that you are living with Ms. Douglas? [Huck nods yes.] And I imagine it was your idea to have me see Huck, Ms. Douglas?

Widow Douglas: Yes. I am really worried about him. He's a poor, lost lamb. His mother is dead. His father, Pap, is the town drunk and hasn't seen Huck for over a year.

Dr. Geigy: And you have taken Huck in?

Widow Douglas: Yes. My sister and I are trying to raise Huckleberry to be a fine boy—to teach him to read and write and learn the Lord's way, but he just does not listen. Last night he ran out and smoked with his no-good friend, Tom Sawyer. He refuses to wear the new clothes I've bought him. And he hates school. Well, I have just about given up hope. I cry; I pray for him all the time, but it does no good.

Dr. Geigy: Hmmm. . . . I see. Any other concerns?

Widow Douglas: Why yes! He told my sister that he wished he could go to hell. He is completely unruly.

Dr. Geigy: I see your concerns. Has Huck ever been to a psychiatrist before?

Widow Douglas: No. . . . [Huck interrupts.]

Huck: And I don't want to be here now! Can we leave, Ms. Douglas?

Widow Douglas: Not yet, Huck. Now sit down and behave or you are going to get a scolding. [Turning her attention to

Dr. Geigy] I read something about ADHD and I wonder if Huck has it. It describes him perfectly—the fidgeting, the wildness. Maybe he has a chemical imbalance and that would explain all this trouble. There's got to be some kind of explanation. He's just not normal. He is a troublemaker. You wouldn't believe the trouble he puts me through. It's not just mischief either. If children behaved like that in my day, their hide got tanned.

Dr. Geigy: Well, let me ask Huck some questions and see. Huck, do you like school?

Huck: No. It's awful dull, specially the books about dead people. I don't take no stock in dead people.

Dr. Geigy: I see. Is it hard for you to pay attention in school?

Huck: Yes, I get all fidgety. I don't see the point of reading and writing.

Dr. Geigy: Is this true, Ms. Douglas? What have you heard from the school?

Widow Douglas: Yes, it's true. His teacher said that he [reading a note from Huck's teacher] "can't stay still in class, lacks interest in homework, interrupts others, and is poor in spelling and math."

Dr. Geigy: And how is home life going for you, Huck?

Huck: Well, the widow is regular and decent, but I can't stand it! Miss Watson is always pecking at me: "Don't put your feet up there, Huckleberry"; "Set up straight"; "Why don't you try to behave?"; "Don't scrunch up like that." I feel so lonesome and tired.

Dr. Geigy: Do you miss your dad?

Huck: Sometimes. He lets me smoke and I don't have to read no books nor study. When I am with Pap, I don't have to be civilized.

Dr. Geigy: Does he ever frighten you?

Huck: Sometimes. I used to be scared of him all the time. He tanned me. I don't miss him much.

Widow Douglas: I worry that Huck is going to be like his dad. Maybe his Pap is ADHD, too.

Dr. Geigy: Getting back to Huck's behavior, how is he at home, Ms. Douglas? You said he doesn't listen to you. Does he fidget?

Widow Douglas: Why yes. Do you think it might be because of his brain? Do you think he has ADHD?

Dr. Geigy: From what the two of you have been saying and the school reports, yes, it sounds like ADHD.

Widow Douglas: What causes ADHD?

Dr. Geigy: Well, research proves that it is a neurobiological or, as you said, a chemical imbalance. Do you know what the treatment is?

Widow Douglas: Is there a medication?

Dr. Geigy: Why yes, Ritalin, or some other psychostimulant. It works on the chemical imbalance. It would help decrease Huck's hyperactivity and improve his ability to pay attention. You know how a diabetic needs insulin? Huck might need Ritalin due to his brain deficiency. From your understanding, has Huck always been this way?

Widow Douglas: Why yes, as far as I know.

Dr. Geigy: I would like to begin a trial of Ritalin to see Huck's response.

Widow Douglas: I have heard some bad things about Ritalin, Doctor. What are the side effects? Should I worry?

Dr. Geigy: No, some of the hype on the risk of psychostimulants is misleading and blown way out of proportion. The most common side effects are loss of appetite, loss of weight, and problems falling asleep. But these are fairly uncommon and are managed effectively by changing the dosage.

Huck: Take a pill? No way! That stuff will just civilize me!

Widow Douglas: Huck, behave. It might help you in school. So you think he has it, Dr. Geigy?

Dr. Geigy: Well, I think so. From the questionnaire [the Connors Rating Scale] that you filled out before coming into my office and your direct report today, yes, I think Huck is ADHD, hyperactive type. [Huck looks sad.] And if he responds to the Ritalin, that will confirm it.

Widow Douglas: Do you have any suggestions for me, Doctor?

Dr. Geigy: Well, you might want to send Huck to a therapist to learn some behavior modification techniques and perhaps take some classes yourself in parenting strategies.

Widow Douglas: Huck, can you leave the office for a minute? [Huck leaves, looking relieved.] Doctor, what do you think of his prognosis? Is there hope?

Dr. Geigy: There is always hope, but what you said about his history of symptoms, his father, and his deceased mother . . . I just don't know. Let's try Ritalin and see. You might want to go to CHADD (Children and Adults with Attention Deficit Disorder). Here's their number.

Widow Douglas: What's CHADD?

Dr. Geigy: It's a support group for parents and caregivers of ADHD kids. They have a lot of information and books you can buy that may help, along with the support.

Widow Douglas: Thanks, Dr. Geigy [breathing a sigh of relief].

[Dr. Geigy writes out a prescription for Ritalin and invites Huck back into the room.]

A Critical Postmortem

What did you think of Dr. Geigy's interview? Did it seem like a fairly sound clinical intervention? It probably was, according to the traditional, medical approach to ADHD. Through that lens, Dr. Geigy's interview was a brief, typical assessment for ADHD, particularly in today's managed care era when time is of the essence. Research confirms that Ritalin is prescribed more frequently for families with managed care plans than for those using other forms of payment (Diller, 1998). The Widow Douglas and Huck's teacher filled out a Connor's questionnaire that confirmed the symptoms of ADHD. Huck's dislike of school and his spontaneous, independent behavior also corroborate the diagnosis. After one expeditious interview, Huck is now "an ADHD kid" on Ritalin.

But was this really a responsible or ethical clinical assessment? Perhaps it would have been if ADHD were a verifiable medical condition. However, a careful analysis of the standard criteria demonstrated in this interview illuminates many troubling issues.

For example, Dr. Geigy refers to ADHD as a neurobiological condition. This is a leap of faith. There is no scientific basis for the widespread belief that ADHD is a neurological defect (Breggin, 1998). In addition, Dr. Geigy's interview barely skims over the context of Huck's life. He doesn't ask about the following:

• *Huck's classroom size or his teacher's pedagogical style.* Perhaps Huck's class, like so many classrooms in today's schools, is overcrowded. Moreover, his teacher's lesson plans may not engage Huck's curiosity or learning style, leaving him vulnerable to distractibility.

• *Facts about his home life.* Dr. Geigy changes the subject when Huck's father is being discussed by saying, "Getting back to Huck's behavior. . . ." By glossing over the effects of Huck's abuse and poverty, he ignores how these contexts might be affecting Huck's ability to concentrate or his preference for action over passivity.

• *The fact that Ritalin improves many people's attention and performance.* An ADHD diagnosis is not needed for the improvement to take place (Diller, 1998). A positive response to psychostimulant medication does not mean that Huck or any other child has ADHD. It only means that Huck, like any other human, is having a predictable and temporary response to a psychostimulant.

- *The possibly harmful side effects.* Dr. Geigy minimized the possibility that Ritalin would have harmful side effects. Long-term effects are not well established (Breggin, 1998).

- *Funding of CHADD by Novartis, the manufacturer of Ritalin* (Breggin, 1998). CHADD's agenda is biased toward viewing ADHD as a disease that requires medication. What would the widow think if she knew that CHADD is influenced by the pharmaceutical company that produces Ritalin? Would she feel there is a potential for conflict of interest?

- *The myth of the so-called "objective" diagnostic standards for ADHD.* Tests such as the Connors Rating Scale are actually subjective and open to interpretation (Breggin, 1998; Diller, 1998; Law, 1997). (In Chapter Two, I discuss the problems regarding the ADHD diagnostic process.)

The Allure of Diagnosing ADHD

Despite these critiques, the diagnosis of ADHD and the prescription for Ritalin appeal highly to parents, teachers, and other interested parties. The Widow Douglas would probably feel relieved to be told that there is a definite, identifiable, scientific cause—a chemical imbalance—for the behavior that causes her so much trouble. Most likely she has been experiencing guilt over the fact that she cannot civilize Huck.

However, Widow Douglas's relief and hope that Huck will change may quickly vanish. She may become disillusioned over time, as Huck's behavior and academic performance fail to improve significantly. Perhaps she will become angry with Dr. Geigy for promising too much. Even more distressing, she may notice herself relating to Huck differently—as a child with a deficit who's incapable of taking responsibility for his own behavior. She had higher expectations of him before the ADHD diagnosis. And all the money she spent on ADHD books may lead to further resentment and hopelessness when Huck's behavior shows little improvement.

In fact, things may ultimately become worse. Although initially relieved, the Widow Douglas may find herself dissatisfied with the effects of Dr. Geigy's treatment of Huck. She may continue to have grave concerns, moreover, about his underlying academic, social, and spiritual development. For, as child psychiatrist Peter Breggin writes, "Ritalin calms children, indeed it often turns rambunctious kids into socially inhibited conformers, which, though it may makes things easier for teachers and parents, is but suppressing the growing-up problems, not solving them" (Breggin, 1998, p. 99).

Impact on the Individual

And what about Huck? Dr. Geigy did not explain to Huck why he should take Ritalin. If Huck had been asked how he felt about being labeled ADHD and taking Ritalin, he probably would have been suspicious, angry, confused, or afraid. He might have begun to think there was something wrong with him because he had to take a little white pill. Maybe Huck would have said that Ritalin made him feel sluggish and tired.

How might the plot of Twain's novel have been different if Huckleberry Finn had been restrained by Ritalin? Would the medication have squashed Huck's spirit, his sense of adventure, his courageous resistance to the culture? Would it, for example, have inhibited his reckless but courageous decision to help his friend Jim, the runaway slave? Their incredibly exciting journey together on the Mississippi River might have never happened. What a boring book that would have been.

What other children in literature could have been chemically altered by an ADHD diagnosis and Ritalin? Huck's friend Tom Sawyer? Holden Caulfield in the *Catcher in the Rye*? Hemingway's Nick Adams? And what about real people who have forever changed the consciousness of our world? If ADHD and Ritalin had been invented earlier, would we have had Leonardo da Vinci's artwork, Maya Angelou's and Earnest Hemingway's writings, Frank Lloyd Wright's architecture, Wolfgang Amadeus Mozart's music, Thomas Edison's inventions, Albert Einstein's genius, or Ted Turner's vision? Each one of these famous and talented people had traits as children that would be described nowadays as hyperactive, inattentive, and impulsive. It is easy to guess that they would be diagnosed in our current biopsychiatric climate as ADHD. Would Ritalin have inhibited their artistry and inventiveness? Would the ADHD label have tricked them into thinking that they were weird or stupid? Would they have been seduced by the ADHD pandemic into believing that they didn't have anything to contribute to society?

These questions leave me with a grave concern: In what way is our current obsession with biopsychiatry preventing future leaders of the twenty-first century from accessing their full creativity by labeling them with a deficit and drugging them with psychostimulant medication?

This book proposes answers to these questions. By critically examining the myths of ADHD, looking at the dangerous effects of the ADHD diagnosis and medication, and offering solutions to problem behavior, I support, defend, and enhance the spirits of children like Huckleberry Finn. Join me on Huck's Mississippi River raft for the next part of the journey: challenging the idea that ADHD is a biological disorder.

Chapter Two

Weird Science

Debunking the ADHD Diagnosis

Interviews like Huck's with Dr. Geigy are commonplace in today's treatment climate. Clinicians are frequently confronted with wild and amazing problems like those described by the Widow Douglas. What may not be apparent to her or to Huck, however, is the intense pressure many clinicians feel to arrive at a diagnosis by the end of a fifty-minute session.

In this climate the number of children and adults diagnosed with ADHD has risen from 900,000 to 5,000,000 since 1990. This dramatic rise in the numbers of ADHD diagnoses is directly tied to another alarming figure—a 700 percent growth in the amount of Ritalin produced in the United States during the same period (Diller, 1998).

Here are some examples from my caseload. I am a family therapist at a large HMO in California. The names and some details of the cases depicted in this book have been changed to protect client privacy.

Eric is a fifteen-year-old boy who has trouble completing his homework assignments. He finds school boring and is more interested in computers, video games, sports, and hanging out with his friends. His grades are B's and C's. Some of Eric's teachers describe him as "distractible." His parents—college professors at the local university— are concerned that his current grade average might keep him from entering a "fine university." They are curious about whether Ritalin might help his concentration and academic performance. Eric, although sensitive to his parents' expectations and concerns, is not at all interested in taking medication; he wonders what it might do to his brain. When I ask Eric what it would mean to take Ritalin, he replies, "It means that I'm crazy."

Susan, a single parent, brings in her two active sons, ages six and eight. As they bounce around my room exploring my toys, puppets, and artwork, Susan describes her recent escape from an abusive relationship. She is finding single parenthood more difficult than she imagined. With further exploration, she wonders if her son's impulsive behavior is due to her poor parenting. Recently the boys' pediatrician suggested they could benefit from Ritalin, stating that their hyperactivity may be genetic and biochemical. Susan has mixed feelings about putting her children on medication but doesn't want to disobey the doctor.

Darrel, a thirty-five-year-old engineer, has recently read a book on adult ADHD and is convinced he has it. He is quite creative at work but has difficulty concentrating and completing all the necessary reading. He wants a referral to a psychiatrist to see if Ritalin will improve his concentration and job performance.

Christine and her eight-year-old son, George, rush into the child social skills group I co-lead. They are late to the group because George has been in a fight during recess at school. She tells me that she will see George's psychiatrist as soon as she can so she can get an adjustment to his dosage of Ritalin.

My caseload is not unique. Across our nation, children and adults bring remarkably similar problems of hyperactivity, oppositionality, and distractibility to therapists for solutions. And with remarkable consistency these problems are labeled ADHD and treated with amphetamines. Given the alarming rate of ADHD diagnoses, you might think there is solid clinical evidence for the condition and its primary treatment, Ritalin. But that's not the case.

In this chapter I examine the evidence for and against the ADHD diagnosis and treatment with Ritalin. I also explore the effects the ADHD diagnosis has on families and therapists. I hope you will find yourself doubting the current "wisdom" that depicts ADHD as a biological condition and will notice the subjectivity of the diagnostic process. By the time you reach the end of this chapter, I hope you'll also arrive at a state of Missouri-style, show-me skepticism. Is ADHD simply like snake oil that's being sold to so many of us?

Current Conventional Wisdom

Most clinicians today would look at the cases like those I described and quickly conclude that these people are ADHD. If clinicians apply the criteria listed in the *Diagnostic and Statistical Manual of Mental Disorders, fourth edition* (DSM-IV), (American Psychiatric Association, 1994), the ADHD child must show some of the defining symptoms of ADHD before the age of seven. Impairments from the symptoms must be present in at least two settings (usually at school and at home). The symptoms also must be present for at least six consecutive months.

The DSM-IV lists full criteria for three discrete types of ADHD: (1) inattentive type, (2) hyperactive-impulsive type, and (3) combined type.

ADHD, Inattentive Type

A child experiencing at least six of the following characteristics will be considered ADHD, inattentive type (American Psychiatric Association, 1994):

- Fails to give close attention to details or makes careless mistakes
- Has difficulty sustaining attention

- Does not appear to listen
- Struggles to follow through on instructions
- Has difficulty with organization
- Avoids or dislikes requiring sustained mental effort
- Often loses things necessary for tasks
- Is easily distracted
- Is forgetful in daily activities

ADHD, Impulsive Type

A young person experiencing six of the following characteristics will be considered ADHD, impulsive type:

- Fidgets with hands or feet or squirms in seat
- Has difficulty remaining seated
- Runs about or climbs excessively
- Has difficulty engaging in activities quietly
- Acts as if driven by a motor
- Talks excessively
- Blurts out answers before questions have been completed
- Has difficulty waiting in turn-taking situations
- Interrupts or intrudes upon others

ADHD, Combined Type

If a child meets the criteria for both the inattentive type and the impulsive type, he or she may be what is called the combined type.

According to the DSM-IV population studies, the diagnosis should occur at a rate of 3–5 percent of the population. The current rate of diagnosis for ADHD far outpaces this epidemiological prediction. In many classrooms, as many as half the boys in the room are taking Ritalin (Diller, 1998). Is it possible that such a huge population of children has a biological disorder? If so many children have this disorder, would you begin to challenge the notion of what a disorder is?

The DSM-IV describes ADHD as a discrete set of symptoms or behaviors that (according to proponents of the disorder) ought to be distinguishable from normal childhood behavior. As I show in detail in the next section, that's an arguable contention. However, researchers have offered numerous theories to explain the genesis of this alleged disorder.

A Brief History of the Diagnosis

Prior to the twentieth century, children's behavioral and attentional problems were described in nonbiological terms. Impulsive or distractible children were thought to have moral or religious defects. This thinking about the cause of children's behavior problems influenced the kind of problem-solving approaches people took. Solutions were located in communities, religious institutions, and families. However, as modern science gradually replaced religion at the center of the emerging American society, these same behavior problems of childhood became medicalized (Cushman, 1995).

The English physician George Frederic Still described one study of children who would fit the modern diagnosis of ADHD as early as 1902 (Armstrong, 1995). In his lectures, Still described twenty children in his practice as aggressive, defiant, and dishonest. Still concluded that these problems were probably hereditary in some children and due to pre- or post-birth injury in others. Instead of locating the children's "moral deficit" in parenting or in religious training deficits, Still attributed the behavior problems to biological conditions resulting from heredity or injury. He also postulated that the problems were chronic in nature (Diller, 1998). His ideas, particularly regarding chronicity and inhibition, remain central to current thinking about ADHD.

This linking of children's behavior problems to biological causes received a boost during a major epidemic of encephalitis in 1917 and 1918. Physicians noted that children with the disease often developed postencephalitic symptoms that included hyperactivity, impulsive behavior, and impaired attention—the same three symptoms that now define ADHD (Diller, 1998).

By the 1930s this collection of behavior problems was referred to as "organic drivenness" (Diller, 1998, p. 82) and was believed to result from some kind of brain injury. The 1930s also saw the first use of stimulant medication to control hyperactivity when Charles Bradley prescribed Benzedrine for that purpose (Armstrong, 1995).

In the 1950s the term *minimal brain dysfunction* (MBD) was used to describe "excessive restlessness," "aimless wandering," and "poor ability to sustain interest in activities" (Diller, 1998, p. 52). *MBD* served as an umbrella term for the effects of brain injury on mentally retarded children. Research, however, failed to show evidence of a biological cause. In addition, physicians felt that MBD was too inclusive a term and not useful in prescribing treatment. Thus MBD fell out of favor (Armstrong, 1995).

During the 1960s, researchers continued to look for a biological cause for hyperactivity in children. New terms were used to describe overactivity—*hyperactive child syndrome* and *hyperkinetic reaction of a childhood,* for example. This decade also saw the first use of Ritalin in the treatment of hyperactivity. The cause of the hyperactivity was believed to be related to brain mechanisms but not necessarily brain damage (Diller, 1998).

In the 1970s psychiatrists turned the focus of their research to the study of attention problems. In 1972 the Canadian researcher Virginia Douglas delivered a seminal paper to the Canadian Psychological Association, arguing that deficits in attention were likely to be the real source in many children's behavioral problems rather than hyperactivity. From this research came another new name—*attention deficit disorder.* The American Psychiatric Association (APA) sanctioned this new disease in 1980 in the DSM-III (Armstrong, 1995).

The 1980s witnessed an ever-increasing swell of research on ADD. With the founding of CHADD, the leading self-help group for ADHD, the diagnosis was injected into mainstream culture. In

1994 Hallowell and Ratey's best-selling book, *Driven to Distraction*, along with several magazine articles on ADD, further popularized the notion of ADD in children and even in adults. By the 1990s "ADD had come into its own as the learning disease *du jour* of American culture" (Armstrong, 1995, p. 8). The APA further refined the diagnosis in 1994 with DSM-IV, where it's referred to as ADHD, inattentive type or ADHD, hyperactive-impulsive type. This refinement led to ever-increasing numbers of children being diagnosed with the disorder (Diller, 1998). In addition, increasing numbers of adults have sought psychiatric help for ADHD after reading one of the popular books on the subject or watching a news magazine program on the disorder.

The ADHD epidemic of the nineties has become an industry. There are literally hundreds of books, training programs, and seminars on the subject. Pharmaceutical companies that produce psychostimulants are making huge profits (Breggin, 1998). According to Diller (1998), profits from Ritalin are up 500 percent since 1990. Likewise, thousands of new clients see thousands of therapists that specialize in ADHD treatment. Some specialists travel the country giving workshops to professionals on how to set up an ADHD clinic (Diller, 1998). As profits rise, so does the widespread popularity of the diagnosis.

In summary, ADHD has a rich and storied life in this century, including several name changes. Yet two features remain constant: (1) the trio of symptoms—inattention, impulsivity, and hyperactivity and (2) the cause as biological and in need of medical treatment. ADHD has become as popular as other twentieth-century diseases such as diabetes, polio, and AIDS. Yet, unlike the aforementioned diseases, ADHD has not been proven to have a biological cause.

The Biological Theory

The idea that ADHD is a biological disease predominates among medical researchers and faculty. The leading proponent of this view is Russell Barkley (1990) of the University of Massachusetts

Medical School, who states that Ritalin is the primary treatment for ADHD. In his book, *Attention Deficit Hyperactivity Disorder: A Handbook for Diagnosing and Treatment* (1990), Barkley states that talk therapies are not helpful and may not be necessary at all. He recommends a lifelong treatment using Ritalin for some ADHD patients. Barkley also reassures physicians that they should not feel guilty if their treatment plan does not include psychosocial elements because ADHD is a biological condition and is not caused or (by his logic) treated by psychosocial interventions (Diller, 1998).

Physicians, the media, and patients widely accept the explanation that ADHD is a biological disease. Physicians and managed care organizations have been particularly influenced by the idea because medicating children with Ritalin is more cost-effective and quicker than other forms of treatment. As a result, children diagnosed with ADHD in HMOs are more likely than privately insured children to receive Ritalin as the primary component of their treatment plan (Diller, 1998).

CHADD promotes this biological disease theory. CHADD has grown to several hundred chapters across the United States and has a membership of 35,000 members (Diller, 1998), mostly parents, who have historically been blamed by psychiatry for their children's problems. Understandably, the notion that ADHD has a biological basis provides welcome relief for parental guilt. This absolution from guilt, as well as the benefits of medicalizing ADHD in order to win insurance coverage and disability rights, encourages the member parents of CHADD to embrace a biological basis for ADHD.

A Challenge to the Popular View

Doctors, mental health professionals, teachers, pharmaceutical companies, parents, magazine covers, and myriad other voices support the notion that ADHD is a biological disorder. But ADHD advocates ignore critical data that disprove the biological explanation. A closer examination of the research reveals methodological flaws, errors, and gaps in the data that have been offered to explain ADHD. Ultimately, there is no solid evidence that ADHD is a verifiable biological disease (Breggin, 1998; Diller, 1998). As Gerald Golden (1991) simply states, "Attempts to define a biological basis for ADHD have been consistently unsuccessful" (p. 36).

Faulty Research

Barkley and other ADHD proponents have found support for a biological root for ADHD in the research of Alan J. Zametkin (Zametkin and others, 1990). Zametkin and his colleagues at the National Institute of Mental Health published a landmark article in *The New England Journal of Medicine* that focused on using advanced brain imaging techniques (called position emission tomography or PET scans) to compare brain metabolism between adults with ADHD and adults without ADHD. The study allegedly documented that adults with ADHD metabolize glucose—the brain's main energy source—more slowly than so-called normal adults. This reduced brain metabolism rate was most evident in the part of the brain that is important for handwriting, attention, motor control, and inhibition of responses. This convinced ADHD researchers such as Barkley and Zametkin that ADHD is a neurological deficit that is not caused by environmental factors.

The media picked up on this research and reported it nationally. Zametkin's research began showing up in CHADD newsletters with headlines such as "ADHD: Not a myth: Finally! The proof we can see and understand" ("ADHD: Not a myth!" 1996). Pictures portraying the spread of glucose through the "normal" brain compared to the "ADHD" brain began showing up in CHADD literature and at CHADD conventions and meetings (Armstrong, 1995).

What was *not* reported by the media or promoted by Barkley and the ADHD community was a replication study of ADHD adolescents by Zametkin and others three years later (Zametkin and others, 1993). In this study, no significant differences were found between the brains of so-called ADHD adolescents and the brains of so-called normal adolescents. Thus the landmark evidence that supported the disease theory was never confirmed or replicated. Yet Barkley and ADHD advocates still cite the 1990 research without mentioning that the research fails to meet one of the primary criteria for good science: that the outcome can be repeated.

Even more troubling, researchers have found flaws in Zametkin's methods of analysis in the original 1990 study (Breggin, 1998; Diller, 1998). For instance, a critique of Zametkin's study by researchers at the University of Nebraska points out that the data did not make clear whether the lower glucose metabolism rates found in ADHD brains were a cause or a result of attentional problems. These researchers stated that if a group of subjects were startled and their levels of adrenaline were then measured, adrenaline levels would be high. That does not mean they had an adrenaline disorder. Without looking at the contextual and environmental factors that led to the high levels of adrenaline, it isn't clear what was happening.

Likewise, even if biochemical differences do exist in the "ADHD brain," their cause is unclear. It may be that such differences become problematic only in certain environmental conditions (Armstrong, 1995). Thus, researchers should be more interested in exploring the interaction of different kinds of brain responses to stress, parenting style, classroom structure, teaching style, and other contextual influences rather than searching for the "ADHD brain."

Ritalin's Effects

One of the more commonly held theories about ADHD is that it is caused by a dopamine deficiency in the prefrontal cortex. Dopamine subdues the responsiveness of neurons to new inputs or stimuli (Diller, 1998). Thus the theory suggests that a child with a dopamine shortage will respond too impulsively in situations where there are multiple stimuli. And because Ritalin is known to increase dopamine levels in the brain, the theory would support the contention that Ritalin is the best treatment for ADHD.

The research, however, fails to support this theory (Breggin, 1998; Diller, 1998). For example, the chemical imbalance fallacy was exposed by Judith Rapoport's studies (Rapoport and others, 1978) showing that stimulants affect both symptomatic and asymptomatic subjects. In her research, she gave Dexedrine to both ADHD children and so-called normal children. Rapoport found that both groups responded similarly in improving their attention and controlling their physical activity. This contradicts the notion that ADHD treats a chemical imbalance. Concurrently, Rapoport's work refutes the common misconception that Ritalin works in some paradoxical way to counteract hyperactivity in children (Breggin, 1998). Ritalin has the same euphoric effect on children and adults, symptomatic or asymptomatic. Ritalin makes everyone feel a bit euphoric and helps everyone maintain better attention in the short run. Unfortunately, those effects do not last (Breggin, 1998). Like many recreational drugs, Ritalin (a form of "speed") is a temporary high that quickly dissipates and is highly addictive.

In spite of the failure of the research to support the dopamine deficiency argument, this theory continues to dominate psychiatric discourse. The idea is based on a widely accepted psychiatric premise: if a patient responds to a psychotropic medication, it proves that a chemical imbalance is present. Often psychiatrists use an analogy of insulin dependence to explain this theory to their patients. They suggest that just as insulin helps diabetics regulate their insulin insufficiency, psychotropic medication makes up for a chemical deficiency and restores a patient's chemical balance. Therefore, if a child responds to Ritalin, his hyperactivity must be a result of dopamine depletion (or a deficiency in some other neurotransmitter).

Unfortunately, this argument is misleading. As pediatrician Lawrence Diller (1998) writes, "In fact such improvement on medication says nothing definitive about the cause of a person's problems. If aspirin relieves a headache, we do not necessarily

conclude that the headache was engendered by an aspirin deficiency" (p. 107). Nevertheless, many parents remain convinced
that if their child improves on Ritalin, it means the problem is
solely biological.

The Cursory Diagnosis

Even with a lack of solid evidence that ADHD is a verifiable medical condition, researchers have attempted to develop standardized
evaluations to arrive at a diagnosis. The standard evaluation for
ADHD purports to offer a concise, objective assessment of the presence or absence of ADHD symptoms. Researchers benefit from
standardized assessment tools because they want a consistent
method for study. In addition, clinicians have been pressured to
streamline the diagnostic process (Breggin, 1998). The influences
of managed care, with its omnipresent focus on time and money,
have forced many clinicians to make rapid-fire diagnoses, often
after one brief intake session.

The standard ADHD evaluation includes child rating scales,
such as the Conners Rating Scale (Conners, 1989), face-to-face
interviews, and intelligence tests. The commonly held belief is that
these diagnostic tools lend themselves to greater objectivity. However, this notion leaves out the underlying lack of scientific evidence
that the condition under examination even exists as a discrete biological entity.

Nevertheless, even if the diagnosis were biological and verifiable, the assessment process is fraught with subjectivity. Questionnaires such as the Conners test ask the raters, usually teachers and
parents, to determine the frequency of problematic behaviors from
a standardized list. Teachers and parents are asked to rate a child on
the scale from 0 (not true at all) to 3 (very much true) in terms of
behavioral statements such as

- Inattentive, easily distracted
- Short attention span

- Restless in the squirmy sense
- Loses temper

How many four-year-olds does that describe? How many eight-year-olds?

An overall score is determined from the answers. If the score is above a certain cutoff point (which represents one standard deviation from the norm), the child meets the ADHD diagnostic criteria. Although these tests may help streamline the process and thus help researchers, the ADHD diagnostic process remains arbitrary. The following are what I see as the most troublesome aspects of the diagnostic process.

The Subjectivity of ADHD

One of the biggest problems with these scales is that they depend on the subjective biases of teachers and parents to rate a child's behavior. Teachers and parents may have some investment in the outcome of the test. Furthermore, because these rating scales depend on opinion rather than fact, there is no objective anchor to decide how much a child is exhibiting ADHD symptoms. As therapist Ian Law (1997) writes, "Two people can observe exactly the same behavior, use exactly the same behavior rating scales, and reach entirely different conclusions" (p. 286).

One study (Reid and others, 1994) found that special education teachers were generally more tolerant of ADHD-type behaviors than mainstream classroom teachers. Wolraich (1996) also demonstrated the subjectivity of raters. He and his colleagues studied teacher rating scales from one year to the next school year. When new teachers were asked to rate children's behaviors, only 52 percent of the same children met the ADHD criteria. The researchers could not account for this drop by comparing it to the child's Ritalin dosage. In contrast, the results of Wolraich's research clearly point to the fact that symptoms are in the eye of the beholder.

The Role of Environmental Factors

To categorize children as ADHD ignores the fact that their problem behavior is the same as that exhibited by children who experience child abuse, trauma, and domestic violence (Breggin, 1998). Other environmental factors such as classroom and teaching style, child-teacher ratios, learning styles, parenting, and stress tend to be glossed over in the traditional diagnostic assessment of ADHD. However, the traditional model, with its individual, biological focus, erases the influence of these contextual factors and places the evaluation of child pathology in the hands of adults who may also be experiencing (or in some cases delivering) the effects of these contexts. Rarely in the traditional diagnostic process are such questions asked as

> How large is this child's classroom?
>
> What is the teacher's predominant teaching style?
>
> Has the child experienced stressful school experiences such as excessive homework, student-teacher conflict, undisciplined classrooms, wetting him- or herself at school, and so on?
>
> Does this child have a history of trauma or abuse?
>
> Is this child currently experiencing trauma or abuse?
>
> Has the child witnessed someone else's suffering inflicted by a serious illness or injury?
>
> Is this child getting breakfast before coming to school?
>
> Does this child have secure housing?
>
> Is this child living in poverty?
>
> Has the child experienced racism, sexism, religious persecution, or homophobia?
>
> Does the child or someone in the child's family experience substantial limitation secondary to a physical or other disability?
>
> Is this child experiencing the effects of drug or alcohol misuse or abuse?

How much television is this child watching?

Has the child recently watched any television shows that may have contributed to fear or restlessness?

Is the child in a blended family, receiving contradictory parenting practices?

Has the child recently moved?

These questions may lead adults to reflect differently on the many possible causes of ADHD-like symptoms. Research confirms that environmental factors can produce symptoms such as restlessness, hyperactivity, inattention, and distractibility (Breggin, 1998). Unfortunately, neither the DSM-IV nor biological explanations for ADHD invite clinicians to explore these divergent and multiple causes.

Cultural Bias

In addition to ignoring environmental factors, ADHD questionnaires and rating scales are based on norms from a white, middle-class bias (Diller, 1998). Criteria such as "restless" and "fidgety" mean different things to different ethnic, racial, and socioeconomic communities. It is possible that these diagnostic tools result in an overrepresentation of poor, nonwhite racial and ethnic groups among children diagnosed with ADHD.

For example, Huck Finn was a poor, white Southern boy with an alcoholic father and an absent mother. By virtue of his membership in a socioeconomic cultural subgroup, he wasn't accepted by the conventional, church-going society of his time. His behavior may have been viewed as marginal, and were he living today it would likely be viewed as evidence for ADHD. There would be little examination of the effects of poverty, trauma, and male training on Huck's behavior. Instead of examining the possible effects that cultural bias may have on producing symptoms such as hyperactivity, these studies locate the problem solely in the brain, devoid of context.

We've already guessed that if Huck were alive today he probably would be diagnosed ADHD. But what if Huck were a member of an ethnic or racial minority? What if Huck's parent were addicted to illegal drugs such as crack or heroin instead of alcohol? Given these indicators, Huck's diagnosis would much more likely be oppositional defiant disorder, or even conduct disorder, on its way to becoming antisocial personality disorder. My point is this: these diagnoses are often shaped by racism, sexism, classism, and the myriad ways oppression filters our perceptions of behavior.

Social and Political Pressures

The DSM-IV is viewed by ADHD advocates as an objective diagnostic manual. However, historical evidence contradicts this notion and illuminates the idea that what gets defined as a disorder is shaped by sociopolitical factors (Caplan, 1995; Kirk and Kutchins, 1992). For example the DSM classified homosexuality as a disorder until 1974, when pressure from gay and lesbian advocates led to removal of homosexuality as a category of disease.

It is fair to conclude that special interests shaped the ADHD criteria that were chosen for DSM-IV. According to Diller (1998), the original ADHD task force determined that only five of the nine symptoms would be required in order to qualify for a diagnosis of ADHD of the hyperactive-inattentive type. However, the DSM-IV supervisory task force overruled this decision and increased the number of symptoms required to six. The DSM committee was worried that five criteria would be viewed as too few and might result in the overdiagnosing of ADHD. Yet the decision to include six rather than five indicators has less to do with science than with bias.

Need for Quick Judgment

Given pressures from managed care and other third-party payers, practitioners often feel justified in diagnosing a child ADHD without a comprehensive assessment. Even though the traditional literature encourages professionals to take their time during the evaluation phase (Barkley, 1990), research shows that, in practice, clinicians are frequently rushed to make important diagnostic conclusions.

In one study, children were diagnosed with ADHD after the therapist briefly interviewed the parent over the telephone (Biederman and others, 1995). Frequently, psychiatrists meet with the parents, but the child is never seen because he or she is viewed as an unreliable historian. I imagine this may be experienced by consumers of our industry—parents and children—as a bit like going to the drive-up window and ordering up a quick fix for an immediate problem—probably not what the family would prefer but the best choice, given the alternatives. The increasing trend of "fastfood" ADHD assessments can lead to ethical dilemmas and liability issues.

Effects of the ADHD Diagnosis on Families and Professionals

Some parents of children who receive the diagnosis of ADHD characterize the diagnosis as liberating and empowering. The notion that a child's problems are not of the parents' own making but due to the child's faulty chemistry provides relief from blame and guilt, along with access to treatment and support. Given the increasing cultural trend to medicalize problems, ADHD as biological entity gives the condition cultural status. Parents can temporarily find comfort in giving a medical name to their child's behavior problems. Once their child has a diagnosis of ADHD, the parents can seek support from CHADD, which further reduces isolation. At self-groups such as CHADD, parents feel understood and accepted. Many parents find emotional strength in sharing experiences and power in CHADD's organized numbers. The child who is diagnosed with ADHD is no longer described as lazy, stupid, or dumb. Furthermore, once the child is labeled ADHD, many educational and psychiatric services are made available to the child and family. And finally, stimulant medication does appear to improve a child's attention, at least in the short run (Griffith and Griffith, 1994).

I acknowledge the possible merits of the established psychiatric approach to ADHD. However, I believe the diagnosis can have insidious effects for children, families, and professionals. This harmful consequence is rarely, if ever, discussed in the traditional ADHD literature. Joining the ADHD bandwagon means swearing devotion to biopsychiatry and the limits of the medical model. I turn to that discussion now.

Stigmatizing Effects on Children

George, who was ten, came into my office with his mother reluctantly. It was clear by the anguished look on his face that he would rather be anywhere else, including a dentist's office. I asked George why he came to see me, and he replied, "I don't know." After several rounds of blank stares and "I don't knows," he said he was ADHD. When I inquired as to what he knew about ADHD, he contritely replied, "I don't know. . . . My mom says I have it, and it means I take this pill. I don't do well in school because I have it."

"Does the pill help?" I asked.

"I don't think so, but I don't know. I mean, it didn't help when I got in a fight the other day and got suspended."

"What happened in the fight?"

"Oh, this kid was calling me names. I couldn't control myself. I'm ADHD. I can't help it. I can't do anything about it. I can't control my temper."

I realized that I needed to change the subject because George really didn't have much sense of personal agency. I decided to focus on his strengths: "George, what are you good at? What are you apart from this ADHD thing?"

"Not much," he answered uneasily.

Mom popped in at this moment. "George, you are good at a lot of things: baseball, Nintendo, helping your dad fix stuff. And you are a great artist."

This interchange is very common in my office. Typically, the child does not want to be seen in therapy. Most children, in my experience, do not identify with the ADD label or understand it. Some use ADHD as an excuse, abdicating responsibility for behaviors that may be under his or her control. Diller (1998) refers to studies that children with ADHD labels tend to hold themselves less accountable for their behavior than other children.

I believe that the ADHD diagnosis can have a totalizing and narrowing effect on a child's life (Nylund and Corsiglia, 1996). The child's ADHD label may invite parents and professionals to develop a deficit view of the young person. Hubble and O'Hanlon (1992) state that labels stick to persons like "crazy glue" (p. 26). For instance, once a child is labeled ADHD, he or she may not be able to enter the armed services because ADHD is considered a disability. Events and behaviors that fall outside the ADHD diagnosis (times when the child was capable and less distracted) may go unnoticed by parents and teachers.

Similarly, parents and teachers also tend to have lowered expectations of children once they are diagnosed as ADHD. Armstrong (1995, pp. 22–23) writes:

> The ADD label creates unintended side effects that are anything but positive. Research over the past twenty-five years has consistently supported the existence of what has been called the self-fulfilling prophecy. That is, what you expect from a child you often get as a result of your expectations. Thus, if you expect a child to do well, then the child will tend to rise to your high expectations. On the other hand, if a parent or teacher sees a child as [having a] disorder (for example, ADD), then the child will tend to modify his behavior to meet that expectation.

Given that language shapes our reality, I am concerned with the deficit language of traditional ADHD discourse. For instance, ADHD proponent Russell Barkley states, "There is, in fact, something *wrong* with these children" (1990, p. 4). What if an ADHD child read Barkley's quote? How would that shape his or her identity? This language of disease and deficiency excludes any talk of children's skills and talents, even though research proves the coincidence of ADHD and creativity (Cramond, 1995). In George's case, the child was unable to access any of his abilities. It seemed clear to me that the ADHD label invited George into a "less than whole" version of himself. In future sessions with George, he was able to re-member (reconnect with his forgotten talents) his abilities that stood outside the ADHD story.

The ADHD assessment process can also be an emotional and stigmatizing one to young persons (Nylund and Corsiglia, 1994). The psychologist often fails to explain to children why they are being tested. Diagnosed ADHD, Erin described her experience of the testing process: "It was horrible. . . . I was ten years old at the time when the school thought I had ADHD. They sent me to be tested. Nothing was explained to me. They [the psychologist and psychiatrist conducting the tests] also weren't very nice! It was scary! I thought I was dying" (Erin, personal communication, 1994).

Physical Effects of Ritalin

As a therapist I often work in collaboration with other professionals (including psychiatrists) to complete my client's treatment plan. The treatment plan for Shawn, an eleven-year-old boy whom I, along with a psychiatrist, was treating for ADHD, inattentive type, typifies this experience. The psychiatrist recommended medication for Shawn, whereas I worked to put ADHD in context and to marshal the family's other resources to limit the effects of ADHD symptoms on their lives. When I asked the doctor how Shawn was responding to Ritalin, he replied, "I think fairly good . . . at least according to the teacher and his mother." I wondered silently to myself if Shawn thought the medication was helpful. The next time I saw him, Shawn said that he didn't like the Ritalin because it made him feel sluggish and tired. He also said it wasn't helping him concentrate.

A substantial number of children I see are never asked how the Ritalin is affecting them. When they are asked, a sizable number respond, just the way Shawn did, that Ritalin makes them feel tired but doesn't seem to do much else. Psychiatrist Peter Breggin (1998) states that parents and professionals are often unaware of the possible permanent damage to the child's brain from the long-term use of psychostimulants. Much of this research has been suppressed or ignored. According to Breggin, the damaging effects of stimulant drugs include

- Decreased blood flow to the brain
- Disruption of growth hormones, leading to suppression of growth in the body and brain of the child
- Permanent neurological tics
- Addiction and abuse, including withdrawal reactions on a daily basis
- Psychosis, depression, mania, irritability, insomnia, and social withdrawal
- Possible shrinkage of the brain
- Decreased appetite and weight loss

Even though Ritalin improves children's attention in the short run, research shows that Ritalin does not promote long-term academic success. In truth, symptoms such as hyperactivity and inattention worsen over time rather than improve (Breggin, 1998). Even the company that produces Ritalin says, "Sufficient data on safety and efficacy of long-term use of Ritalin in children are not yet available. Long-term effects of Ritalin in children have not been well established" (Breggin, 1998, p. 99).

In addition to the physical side effects of the medication, I am concerned about the psychological effects. For example, the power imbalance between the physician, the family, and the child may marginalize the parents' and child's concerns and experiences, as well as their own knowledge of solutions. Often the doctor offers simplistic and deficit-saturated explanations regarding the rationale for taking Ritalin. The chemical imbalance notion may invite families to depend too much on the drug for the entire solution (Nylund and Corsiglia, 1996). Correspondingly, parents of children diagnosed with ADHD may have unrealistic expectations about what the medication can accomplish because of clinicians' "promising too much" (Griffith and Griffith, 1996, p. 202). These unrealistic expectations often lead to disappointment.

A loss of personal agency may be another effect of overemphasis on medication therapy. As Griffith and Griffith express, "For many, taking a medication evokes images of weakness, loss of responsibility, and submission to medical authorities. Historically, these are attributions that have closely accompanied the sick role in American culture. These associations can invite an emotional posture of submission that obscures a patient's awareness of life choices to the patient's detriment" (p. 199). On innumerable occasions, a child describes the stimulant medication as the sole reason for his or success while undermining his or her abilities, talents, motivation, and creativity.

Effects on Parents

Jenny was a thirty-three-year-old single parent who was concerned that her son, Tyler, was exhibiting some symptoms of ADHD. As a third grade school teacher, Jenny was well versed in the signs of ADHD. After all, during countless parent-teacher conferences, Jenny had suggested to other parents that they might consider taking their child to a physician for an ADHD evaluation. Now she was receiving feedback from Tyler's second grade teacher that he was restless, inattentive, and hyper. Grudgingly, Jenny admitted that Tyler also exhibited these symptoms at home. According to the Connors Rating Scale, Tyler warranted a diagnosis of ADHD, hyperactive type. Subsequently, Jenny took her son for an evaluation in the pediatrics department. After a fifteen-minute interview, Tyler was diagnosed with ADHD; the doctor recommended Ritalin.

Jenny was hesitant to start Tyler on Ritalin, as she had heard about some of its potentially damaging side effects. It was one thing to recommend medication for other children; to recommend it to her son was another thing entirely. The pediatrician then suggested she refer Tyler to me for therapy. The doctor also encouraged Jenny to take an ADHD class for parents so that she could get more information on the "disorder."

Three weeks later I met Tyler and Jenny for the first time. Jenny had been attending the ADHD parenting classes. I asked her what she thought of the class. Jenny replied, "Well, I like the information and the support . . . but some of the ideas and the way that some of the parents talk about their kids doesn't fit for me. They all seem so pessimistic . . . like, their kids are damaged. I don't like that."

"What don't you like about it?" I asked.

"Since this whole ADHD things got started, I find myself expecting less from Tyler," she said.

"What do you mean?" I inquired.

"Well, I don't ask him to do chores now or require him to do his homework by himself. . . . I used to before ADHD."

"Does the idea that Tyler is ADHD contribute to an idea that he's less capable? That he has to settle for less in life?"

"Yeah, I think so," Jenny said, as she was beginning to get a new perspective on the ADHD label. She went on to say that although some of the strategies the instructor taught were interesting, they didn't work for her. She began to doubt her own skill as a parent. Jenny felt that if she didn't follow through with the instructor's ideas she would be considered noncompliant.

Later on in the session, Jenny and I talked about medication. She had not decided yet what to do about Ritalin. "I mean, if I don't listen to his doctor's suggestions, I am being a bad parent because I am not getting Tyler the treatment he needs for his condition. But I feel like a bad parent if I do put him on it, given the side effects."

"Does it feel like a no-win situation? Like a parent trap—either way you lose and are a failure as a parent?" I suggested.

I invited Jenny to reconsider the idea that she was a bad parent and to consider that her resistance to medication was a healthy resistance. It meant she wanted the best for Tyler. I also invited Jenny to look at evidence that proved she was a capable parent— that she had used several creative parenting strategies that were effective.

Parents often notice that their expectations become lower after their child is labeled ADHD. The diagnosis may also encourage parents of ADHD children to surrender responsibility for aspects of their children's problems that could be managed and changed. I agree with family therapist Brain Cade (1990), who states, "It is my opinion that using a diagnosis such as hyperactive is largely unhelpful (unless you manufacture Ritalin, or some other medication) and often leads to pessimism and resignation on the part of parents" (p. 45). Parents and kids often find themselves blaming ADHD for problems rather than joining together to find solutions.

Some other conventional therapy practices such as psycho-education and behavior therapy can also lead to potential problems. Traditional behavior therapy and psychoeducation can be highly prescriptive instead of collaborative. The clinician, from a position of expertise, instructs the parents as to what will be useful with their "ADHD child." Although any of these techniques may be useful, the suggestions are often unsolicited and can be experienced by parents as judgmental. Frequently, the suggestions presume there is one correct way to parent children, particularly ADHD children. This presumption easily invites parents to doubt their own abilities and parenting preference. The resulting self-doubt can lead to parenting paralysis. Moreover, if the parent does not follow through with the therapist's directives, the parent is (as Jenny feared) viewed as resistant. This one-way process of therapy replicates the parent trap and discounts parents' own unique knowledge that may help their child.

Therapist Resignation

A couple of years ago, a colleague of mine was in a dilemma. She had been asked to teach the ADHD class for parents. Because it was a job requirement at the HMO where we work, she couldn't refuse. She liked teaching classes, but she was uneasy with the content of the course, which included behavior therapy, the concept of ADHD as a biological entity, and medication as the primary treatment. The ideas contradicted her preferred views and theoretical orientation, which is more similar to mine. She felt the class's material recruited her into a therapeutic straightjacket that limited her repertoire. Instead of collaborating with the parents, the syllabus encouraged her to teach the class from a didactic point of view. Even though she didn't prefer this way of teaching, she noticed that over time she became captivated by the traditional ADHD ideas. In her individual therapy practice, she began experiencing cynicism with her ADHD cases. This pessimism led to the loss of her usual therapeutic creativity with families. Instead of working to empower the family and child, she referred them to the psychiatrist and class, implying that talk therapy probably wouldn't be helpful for ADHD. She had been indoctrinated by the traditional ADHD discourse. Like parents, treating professionals can also be tricked by the ADHD discourse into pessimism and the reduction of complex problems into a simple, biology-plus-medication formula that does not spell success for kids and families.

The ADHD diagnosis recruits therapists into resignation. In addition, the seduction of the diagnosis can tempt therapists to take an "expert position" with the families they attempt to help. What's wrong with expecting therapists to be experts? After all, that's what they're paid for, right? Actually, the expert position has numerous pitfalls for both therapists and the families they treat. Therapists who embrace expertise become convinced that their ADHD assessment is real, true, and objective (Nylund and Corsiglia, 1996). Hubble and O'Hanlon (1992) refer to this occurrence as "delusions of certainty" (p. 26). Once the therapist becomes the expert, the client's knowledge is diminished. The pressure is on the therapist to have all the right answers. Simultaneously, the pressure is on the family to be receptive to the therapist's suggestions and to "perform" better so that the therapist maintains his or her expertise. But what happens if the therapist's suggestions assume a single cause for a complex problem? What if the solutions or parenting models generate from a different cultural location than the one inhabited or preferred by the family? What if the family has vast resources that are unnoticed and untapped by the treating therapist? In my experience, the talents and creative responses of families far outnumber the tricks of ADHD and the simple, mechanical approaches to parenting offered by traditional family therapy models.

Law (1997) asked therapists some very astute questions regarding the predicament that my colleague (and many other therapists) experienced:

> How, as family therapists, did we respond before ADD was invented? Did we not attempt to put the presentation of any given problem into a context? Were we not aware that some children, especially boys, were vulnerable to reproducing male violence and aggression when they had been subjected to abuse and violence in their lives, particularly by men? Were we not aware of the ways in which children expressed emotional distress and of how these expressions were experienced and described by parents and professionals as "behavior problems?" If children had learning difficulties, did we not have ways of assessing and naming those and providing additional learning supports without pathologizing and infantilizing the children? What does the invention of a new pathology give us that we did not have access to before? If psychostimulants have an effect on us all, regardless of diagnosis, why does the use of medication need to be predicated on children being defined as neurologically and psychologically "less than"? [pp. 302–303].

Moving On to Solution Land

We've come to a turning point on our journey. Some folks will continue down the traditional path toward the ADHD diagnosis, Ritalin treatment, and cognitive-behavioral approaches to parenting. Others will take a critical view of the landscape and will notice some important features of the ADHD terrain.

For example, some will focus on the lack of scientific evidence for ADHD and the potential personal and social consequences of mass prescriptions of psychostimulants. Others will notice the many contextual factors that affect and explain the presentation and diagnosis of ADHD symptoms. Many will be intrigued by the possibility of a treatment methodology that combats parent, child, and professional burn-out and offers a sound alternative to Ritalin.

For those of you who want to explore some new waters, it's time to direct our attention to therapeutic solutions that move beyond deficit and disorder and toward hope and possibility. There is a wide strait in the river of optimism and imagination that Huck would want us to discover. Let's row ahead and point our oars in the direction of solutions.

Part Two

The Solution

Chapter Three

The SMART Approach

An Overview

In Part One of the book we explored the creation and expansion of the ADHD diagnosis in the United States. We noted the paucity of scientific evidence for the disorder and the potentially harmful effects of Ritalin—the medicine most prescribed for the treatment of ADHD. We concluded that if Huck Finn were alive today, he would probably meet the diagnostic criteria for ADHD and find himself taking Ritalin, with devastating consequences for his creativity, conscience, courage, and development.

Several leading physicians and clinicians now critique the ADHD phenomenon (Breeding, 1996; Breggin, 1998; Diller, 1998). As I join in their critique of the ADHD diagnosis, I want to make clear that I do not discount the gravity of ADHD symptoms; they can have a devastating impact on children, parents, families, schools, and communities. The symptoms include violence and aggression; oppositionality, distraction, and disruption in the classroom; expulsion; social isolation; difficulties getting along with other children; and defiance of teachers and parents. ADHD symptoms leave parents and families feeling powerless, hopeless, and judged.

Neither do I intend to minimize the problems suffered by children with ADHD by referring to them as more spirited or energetic than other children. Nevertheless, I remain unconvinced by the ADHD-Ritalin marketing position that the cause of ADHD symptoms is simply biological and that its treatment is simply pharmaceutical. The public discourse on ADHD has focused on a debate between those who view ADHD as a biological condition and those who view it solely as a social condition. Buchanan and Stayton (1994) refer to this either-or debate as "pejorative dualism." (I think there is a more helpful way of understanding ADHD. Moving beyond a reductive, either-or distinction, I understand ADHD as a construct that is produced in a social context, which may include institutional, interpersonal, and biological factors. This view makes room for a wide range of solutions to ADHD symptoms and behavior problems.

I could go on talking about the problem of ADHD for quite awhile. In my experience, clinicians are pretty good at what family therapist David Epston (1993, p. 163) refers to as "problem talk." Epston has observed at traditional case conferences (where interdisciplinary teams of mental health professional meet to discuss clients) that clinicians spend most of their time describing a client's problem, hypothesizing about the origins of the problem, and examining the operation of the problem in the client's life. Very little time is spent on solution talk—what the client or the clinician might do to solve the problem. According to family therapists Furman and Ahola (1992), solution talk is "achieved by thinking positively and by focusing on subjects that foster hope, such as resources, progress, and the future" (p. xxiv).

I think Huck would approve of solution talk; he was a solution-focused character. He didn't spend his time talking about problems. He solved them. Taking a cue from Huck, this book is significantly weighted toward solution talk. If we all agree that ADHD-like symptoms are a problem, exactly how can we help children find the resources to combat that problem?

In this chapter we turn our attention to the SMART approach to treating ADHD. First, I discuss some of the ideas that have shaped my approach to therapy, including competency-based, postmodern therapies such as narrative therapy, solution-focused therapy, and collaborative language systems (CLS). Next, I provide an overview of basic concepts of the SMART approach. By the end of this chapter you will be ready to get started with SMART therapy. You will understand the guiding attitudes of the SMART therapist and will have keys to unlock the collaborative assessment process, including the SMART rating scale.

Postmodern Therapies

The SMART approach is influenced by postmodern therapies. According to Nichols and Schwartz (1995), postmodernism "views knowledge as relative and context-dependent [and] questions assumptions of objectivity that characterize modern science. . . . In family therapy, [postmodernism refers to] challenging the idea of scientific certainty, and [is] linked to the method of deconstruction" (p. 593).

Traditional therapies emphasize the objective assessment and treatment of scientifically verifiable disorders. In contrast, postmodern therapists believe that disorders such as ADHD are produced in a sociohistorical and political context. There is no absolute or true cause of a problem like ADHD, and such problems do not exist in a vacuum. Instead, problems are shaped by the subjective understandings of the therapist, the client, and the society in which they all live.

This shift from the objective to the subjective point of view has a significant impact on therapy. Traditional ideas seek one cause for a problem like ADHD and promote one solution, like Ritalin. Postmodern therapies reject this one-size-fits-all mode of treatment, preferring instead to tailor treatment to the creativity and resources of clients. In order to accomplish this, postmodern therapists engage in conversational practices that attempt to "deconstruct" or "unpack" taken-for-granted assumptions that define, describe, or support problems. By deconstructing popular and unquestioned ideas, postmodern therapies make room for preferred or more useful meanings about the problem (Freedman and Combs, 1996). For example, postmodern therapies do not accept the notion that ADHD is a fixed biological condition. Instead they see it as a pernicious, overdetermined problem that is amenable to change. Finally, postmodern therapies promote conversations that emphasize the client's own knowledge, experience, and ideas for solutions. Postmodern therapies raise new possibilities for living outside the limiting and deficit-bound descriptions of a problem such as ADHD.

Narrative Therapy

The SMART approach is primarily informed by the narrative metaphor for therapy, including the ideas of Michael White and David Epston (1990) and their colleagues (Freedman and Combs, 1996; Freeman, Epston, and Lobovits, 1997; Madigan, 1996; Monk, Winslade, Crocket, and Epston, 1997; Smith and Nylund, 1997; Zimmerman and Dickerson, 1996). White and his colleagues have been influenced by scholars from diverse disciplines—postmodern philosophers Michel Foucault (1973) and Jacques Derrida (1981), social psychologist Jerome Bruner (1986), anthropologists Victor Turner and Edward Bruner (1986), and systems theorist Gregory Bateson (1972). From these and other sources, a set of ideas and practices converged to form what is now commonly referred to as narrative therapy.

Narrative therapists believe that human beings live their lives according to stories that reflect the meanings people make of the events they experience. Stories both describe and shape people's lives. According to White and Epston (1990), families and individuals often become bogged down in dominant stories that disqualify, limit, or disempower them. For example, a child who has been labeled ADHD can develop a deficit-based story of himself. The ADHD story becomes dominant and totalizing; the child's past, present, and future are seen through an ADHD lens (for example, "Johnny did that because he has ADHD, and he's going to have it his whole life"). As a consequence parents and teachers may fail to notice events or behaviors in a child's life that contradict the ADHD story. The deficit story frequently becomes internalized so that the name ADHD and the client become one and the same.

Narrative therapists attempt to challenge dominant, problem-saturated stories by engaging clients in externalizing conversations that separate the problem from the person. For example, clients are encouraged to give the problem a name such as the Temper Monster or the Tickles. By discussing the problem itself as the problem rather than the child's biology or disorder as the problem, narrative therapists begin to distinguish between the child's preferred ways of being and the problem's effects on the child. Externalizing conversations make room for the child's abilities, skills, and talents that exist alongside the problem story. These abilities, which may have been previously overlooked or impeded by the problem story, are now fertile ground for developing problem-solving strategies. Externalizing conversations encourage therapists and clients to align with each other and against the problem. Consequently, far from inviting hopelessness or resignation, externalizing conversations promote the child's and the family's agency to fight the problem and its effects.

Once the problem is separated from the person, space is opened for the therapist and the client to attend to experiences or events that challenge the problem story. These events are referred to as unique outcomes or sparkling moments—times when the problem (or the problem story) is not in charge of the client. Questioning and other clinical practices such as letter writing explore the client's understanding of these victories over the problem, thereby thickening the story of the client's success.

I find the narrative metaphor invaluable in therapy. A narrative view of the person suggests to the therapist and the client that everybody lives a multistoried life. This means that all stories are partial; no single story can speak to the totality of a person's lived experience. Narrative therapy helps unearth stories of skill, resiliency, and ability. The deficit, ADHD story is not the only story; stories of creativity and talent also exist in children labeled ADHD. The narrative lens allows me to make use of these stories of competence.

Solution-Focused Therapy

The solution-focused therapy (SFT) model (Berg, 1994; Berg and Miller, 1992; de Shazer, 1985, 1988, 1991, 1994; Miller, Hubble, and Duncan, 1996; O'Hanlon and Weiner-Davis, 1989; Walter and Peller, 1992) has become increasingly popular in the last decade, particularly with managed care health plans, due to its emphasis on brief, measurable, and long-lasting change. Many therapists have learned the model in order to become more cost-effective, goal-directed, and efficient in therapy.

SFT is a user-friendly and practical therapy. Therapists who use this approach ask clients to define their complaint and then search for instances when this complaint is less present in their lives. These instances are referred to as exceptions. The therapist then uses these exceptions to construct a solution by asking carefully crafted questions. One of the best-known techniques is to ask the miracle question: If there were a miracle one night while you were sleeping and the problem was gone when you woke up, how would you know? By imagining the outcome of the miracle in some detail, clients can be more hopeful about the future.

SFT is useful in my work with ADHD children because it helps me focus on exceptions to problems. In addition, SFT techniques enable me to set specific, clear goals with children and families; by setting measurable, achievable goals, positive therapeutic outcomes become more possible.

Collaborative Language Systems (CLS)

CLS therapy is based on the work of Harry Goolishian, Harlene Anderson, and Tom Andersen (Andersen, 1991; Anderson and Goolishian, 1988, 1992; Anderson, 1997). A CLS approach helps clients move from their limited self-perception to a broader view of their situation by engaging them in a therapeutic dialogue. Anderson and Goolishian (1992) assert that in order to more fully facilitate dialogue among family members who may have become monological (family members holding too tightly to one way of viewing the problem situation), the therapist must take a "not-knowing" position. This does not mean that the therapist knows nothing but that the therapist must leave all preconceived assumptions about clients out of the therapy room. This position allows the therapist to be uncertain and in a learning, curious stance.

A CLS therapist allows clients to be at center stage—to lead the story, the way they want to tell it, without being guided by what the therapist thinks is important. The therapist is not necessarily interested in finding a solution to the problem but rather in providing a dialogical atmosphere that allows clients to hear one another and to talk about a problem until the problem dissolves in the emergence of new stories and perspectives.

In true postmodern style, a CLS therapist is able to entertain multiple and contradictory ideas simultaneously. For example, a CLS therapist can respect the idea that ADHD is a biological disorder. So while honoring a client's viewpoint that ADHD is a medical disorder, the CLS therapist can also consider the idea that ADHD is a shoddily built social construct. There is no need to take an either-or position. Both positions (and others) become part of the dialogue.

My work with ADHD children has benefited greatly from CLS. By taking the stance of not knowing, I am able to stay curious and respectful. The CLS approach allows me to be an active listener and to pace the session so the child or parent feels understood. The CLS notion of holding many contradictory ideas concurrently allows me to honor some parents' view that their ADHD children have a medical condition. I feel no need to argue them out of their position. Rather, I listen and respect their meaning of ADHD. Then I carefully and slowly ask questions that suggest new perspectives on ADHD.

The SMART Steps

Informed by the models of therapy I have described, I developed an acronym—SMART—that refers to a five-step narrative approach to treating children labeled ADHD. The five steps are as follows:

Separating the problem of ADHD from the child. SMART therapists engage children and families in externalizing conversations. They separate the problem (ADHD) from the person and give it a name such as the Hyper Monster. The effect of this subtle language shift is that children begin to experience ADHD as coming from a source outside themselves. Space for new perspectives is opened up; blame becomes less important.

Mapping the influence of ADHD on the child and the family. Having named the problem, the SMART therapist asks questions designed to map the influence of ADHD. These questions explore the strength of the problem relative to the strength of the child. The first series of questions maps the influence of ADHD on the person. In the process of answering the questions, the child gains a much richer account of what ADHD has cost him or her and others. The next series of questions probes the child's influence over ADHD.

Attending to exceptions to the ADHD story. The SMART therapist listens carefully to events that stand apart from the ADHD story. These events are referred to as exceptions or unique outcomes. By asking exception questions, the therapist inquires into the child's successful influence over the problem.

Reclaiming special abilities of children diagnosed with ADHD. Exceptions to the ADHD story become an entry point into a new story—one of competence and ability. Questions are asked to thicken the new story. Further questions are asked to detail the history of competence and ability. Once these discoveries are made, children are able to "re-member" their hidden talents and successes.

Telling and celebrating the new story. Because the new story needs to be highlighted, questions are asked by way of reworking the child's reputation. An audience to the changes is deliberately sought out to authenticate and celebrate the new developments in the child's life.

These SMART steps will be illustrated and discussed in much greater detail in subsequent chapters. However, before starting

SMART therapy, I want to discuss the underlying attitudes that inform it.

Guiding Attitudes of the SMART Therapist

SMART therapists are guided by certain attitudes or ethical postures in their work with children. These attitudes help them ask the kinds of questions that create possibilities and open space for new stories, thus providing the groundwork and context for SMART therapy.

Curiosity

As opposed to traditional therapists who operate from a position of expertise and certainty, SMART therapists take a stance of curiosity. This means they privilege children's and their families' expertise about problems and solutions. SMART therapists can tolerate ambiguity and move tentatively in defining the problem. The SMART approach encourages clinicians to avoid the assumption that they understand children's experiences. Instead, therapists remain genuinely inquisitive about their clients' knowledge and understanding. The greatest tool of SMART therapists is questions—questions that are neither designed to diagnose children nor to confirm what therapists already think they know. Rather, the questions are designed to discover the unique struggles, strengths, and abilities of children.

Respect

The SMART therapist has a deep respect for the knowledge of children labeled ADHD. It is imperative to believe that children have hidden resources that have been overlooked or ignored. Often they have not been encouraged to access their own problem-solving abilities because the deficit language of ADHD has subjugated their knowledge; they become convinced—and everyone around them is convinced—that ADHD is in charge. The SMART approach works to resurrect this knowledge and value it over "expert" ideas about ADHD.

SMART therapists do not assume that they know what is best for children or their families. This way of working requires clinicians to be ever vigilant about imposing their own biases; they must frequently check in with the child and family to make sure their meanings are being privileged and respected. Thus the therapy becomes a collaborative endeavor that helps to flatten the hierarchy that exists between client and therapist.

Hopefulness

SMART therapists value curiosity and respect; they remain vigilant about imposing their biases on children and families. However, one bias that SMART therapists persistently introduce into therapy is hope. SMART therapy operates from a place of "tempered optimism" (Winslade and Monk, 1999, p. 28). The diagnosis of ADHD can invite therapists to feel discouraged about the therapeutic prognosis. As stated in Chapter Two, the traditional ADHD belief that the child will have a biological condition for life forces therapists (and children and families) into resignation. SMART therapists do not get recruited into this despair. Using language of hope and possibility, SMART clinicians believe that change is possible and that children have the abilities and resources to solve their own problems. As family therapist Colin Sanders (personal communication, 1998) says, "Language gives us the opportunity to transcend biological fatalism."

The SMART Assessment

With these attitudes—curiosity, respect, and hope—SMART therapists take a unique approach to the assessment phase of treatment. In today's managed care era, most therapists have only one session authorized to develop a diagnosis and treatment plan. They must not only conduct an assessment session in a time-efficient manner but develop treatment goals and plans with children by the end of the first session.

In a majority of my intake interviews, a previous professional (a teacher or pediatrician) has told the parents that their child is ADHD and needs an evaluation conducted by a therapist to confirm the diagnosis. Medication has usually been recommended or started. Early in the first session, the parent typically asks me to verify the ADHD diagnosis. Usually I respond by saying, "I am not sure. I need to ask more questions. Would that be OK? I need to conduct an assessment to see what is going on and what might be helpful."

However, as a SMART therapist, my ADHD assessment is quite distinct from the traditional evaluation (see Table 3.1). I employ a collaborative and strengths-based approach (Selekman, 1997) to the assessment process to avoid reproducing the problems inherent in the conventional diagnostic process. Instead of conducting an assessment inquiry that operates from a place of expertise and aims at finding the "truth," I strive to privilege the child's and family's unique sociocultural situation and their own understanding of their concerns (Smith, 1997). By the end of the first session, I co-formulate treatment goals with the family, and we are ready to move toward the first step in the SMART approach.

The SMART assessment format consists of five areas of therapeutic inquiry and collaboration: (1) the meanings the family makes of ADHD, (2) the environmental checklist, (3) the SMART rating scale, (4) collaborative goal setting, and (5) the medication option. I will discuss each of these areas in detail.

The Meanings the Family Makes of ADHD

Instead of being preoccupied with the etiology of ADHD, I am interested in what ADHD means to the child and the family. Through a collaborative inquiry, family stories about ADHD and medication are explored. I am particularly interested in the family's understanding

**Table 3.1 The Traditional Assessment
Versus the SMART Assessment.**

	Traditional ADHD	SMART Assessment
Purpose	Diagnosis and classification	Problem solving finding strengths
Criterion	The ADHD child is seen as the problem.	ADHD symptoms are seen as the problem, not the child.
Methods	Standardized tests, such as the Connors Rating Scale, are designed to diagnose and classify the child according to norms. The testing highlights the child's deficits.	Collaboration conversations occur with the therapist, the child, and the parents. The conversations focus on what ADHD symptoms mean to the family, the effects of ADHD symptoms, and the environmental influences that may be supporting the problem. A rating scale (the SMART scale) is used to highlight the child's strengths.
Product	A report is made containing the evaluator's diagnoses, deficit interpretations, and recommendations. It is released to the child and family reluctantly, if at all. Report is written in professional language from an "expert" position.	The child's strengths are identified. In addition, the family selects goals for treatment. If a report is made, it is co-written with the family and written in nonexpert, everyday language.
Criterion	Is viewed as an "objective" assessment	Does not pretend to be objective. Data are used only to generate solutions.

of ADHD and how sources of information (such as books, magazines, school, and other parents) have contributed to their awareness.

Often parents have found the diagnosis (and dominant ideas about ADHD) helpful; ADHD relieves their sense of guilt. My intention is to collaborate with parents, so I do not try to argue them out of their construction of the problem. To challenge their perspective at this point in therapy would only invite defensiveness on their part.

With regard to respecting the parent's point of view, Ian Law (1997) writes:

> Taking a critical position in relation to the dominant medical and psychological discursive construction of ADD (ADHD) and tackling it head on can seem a bit like stepping out in front of a big truck with arms raised, carrying a little red sign with the word "stop" written on it. You are liable to get run over. So when a therapist is working with families that have already been enlisted into the ADD discourse and have a belief in the diagnosis and the efficacy of medication, arguing against the belief or attempting to deconstruct the notion without the preparation of an acceptable alternative understanding is likely to increase any sense of guilt frustration, or hopelessness that made them so vulnerable to accepting the "biological basis of behavior" construct in the first place [p. 296].

Hence, instead of ending up in a debate with parents, I maintain of stance of not knowing and of curiosity. This stance allows me to ask questions such as

To the Parents

- What is your understanding of ADHD?
- How did you learn about ADHD?
- Has the diagnosis been helpful?
- What is now possible that wasn't possible before your child was diagnosed ADHD?

- What are the limitations of the ADHD diagnosis?
- How (if the child is on medication) has the medication helped, and what behaviors does it seem not to help?
- What are some of the qualities your child possesses that are separate form ADHD?

To the Child Labeled ADHD

- Do you know what ADHD stands for?
- What does ADHD mean to you?
- Do you know why you are taking medication?
- Is Ritalin helpful?
- Who are you separate from ADHD?

These questions respect the family's perspective but also open up space for them to separate themselves from the taken-for-granted views of ADHD. The questions also begin the process of deconstruction, which will be further explored in step 2 of the SMART approach. Last, the questions provide useful information about the parents' unique meanings of ADHD. Some parents do not find the diagnosis useful, and thus we move on rather quickly to what they would like help with. The ADHD diagnosis is rendered irrelevant in these instances. In these situations, therapy tends to be brief. With parents who have invested in the pathologizing ideas of ADHD, the information they provide tells me that therapy will go slower. In these cases I remind myself to be patient in helping parents and children stand against the effects of pathologizing, blaming, and labeling.

The Environmental Checklist

In the first session, I like to inquire about the possible stressors that may be occurring in the child's environment. Instead of a symptom checklist that focuses on the child's so-called medical disorder, I use an environmental checklist to examine the child's context. Research demonstrates that a number of stressors and environmental factors contribute to symptoms such as hyperactivity and inattention (Breggin, 1998). If I use the DSM checklist as my guide during the assessment phase of treatment, I might miss important contextual data. Here are the questions I include in a first interview:

Is this child currently experiencing trauma or physical, sexual, or emotional abuse in the family by parents or siblings?

Does this child have a history of trauma or abuse?

Has the child witnessed a family member's suffering inflicted by a serious illness or injury?

Has there been domestic violence in the home?

Is the child receiving contradictory parenting practices?

Have there been major changes in the family structure (new sibling, remarriage)?

Is the child receiving enough attention from his or her parents?

What stressors are the parents experiencing (work stress, substance misuse, unemployment)?

Does the child or someone in the child's family experience substantial limitation secondary to a physical or other disability?

Has there been a recent divorce in the family?

How does the child's behavior compare to his or her siblings' behavior?

Is this child experiencing the effects of drug or alcohol misuse or abuse?

How much television is this child watching?

Has the child recently watched any television shows that may contribute to fear or restlessness?

Has the child recently moved?

How large is this child's classroom?

What is the teacher's predominant teaching style?

Has the child experienced stressful school experiences such as excessive homework, student-teacher conflict, undisciplined classrooms, and wetting him- or herself at school?

Does this child have secure housing?

Is this child living in poverty?

Has the child experienced racism, sexism, religious persecution, or homophobia?

Has the child experienced a recent catastrophic event such as floods, hurricanes, or street violence?

These questions provide me with much richer information than the checklist would. If the child is experiencing one or more of the situations or stressors, I tell the parent that there may be more than one cause of their child's behavior, not just a "brain disease." I invite the parent to begin looking for clues that may indicate other potential influences on the child's behavior, either positively or negatively. Work then begins on modifying the child's environment.

For example, with Gene, age ten, who was referred to me for hyperactivity and inattention, I asked several of the questions. I discovered that the symptoms began soon after his parents had separated. In private Gene told me that he worried his father would never visit him. I shared his worry with his father, John. In response, John assured his son that he would see him frequently. Soon after this conversation his so-called ADHD symptoms subsided.

The SMART Rating Scale

Frequently, in the first interview the parent and teacher have already filled out a symptom checklist (such as the Connors Rating Scale). To counter the pathologizing effects of these rating scales, I ask the parents and the child's teacher to fill out a rating scale I developed—the SMART scale (there is a separate questionnaire for parents and teachers). This scale is a subjective questionnaire to identify a child's strengths and abilities; it helps me get to know the child apart from the ADHD-deficit story. I do not view the questionnaire as an objective measurement of the child but a tool in therapeutic conversations to elicit and promote the child's preferred abilities, stories, and competencies. Parents and teachers respond positively to my rating scales. Our medicalizing culture tends to give weight to such questionnaires. The SMART scales use this cultural practice to give credibility to a child's abilities and resources. For example, if the child scores a number of 2's (pretty much true) and 3's (very much true) on the scale, I use it as an opportunity to develop an alternative, competency-based narrative for the child. (In Chapter Seven I focus on building an alternative story.) As Freeman, Epston, and Lobovits (1997) write, "Getting to know the young person apart from the problem can give us coordinates and set us on a playful adventure of change. Specific knowledge of her [his] interests and abilities tells us what a child might bring to put against the problem. Having this knowledge, the therapist then joins the child in conversation, providing linguistic bridges that enable her to tackle the problem in her own imaginative way" (p. 37). I have included an example of a SMART rating scale for teachers and parents (shown in Exhibit 3.1 and Exhibit 3.2).

Using the SMART Rating Scale in Therapy

Here's an illustration of using the SMART rating scale in therapy: Lawrence, age eight, was referred to me shortly after being diagnosed ADHD. His teacher had recommended an ADHD evaluation due to his lack of concentration, his hyperactivity, and his temper outbursts in the classroom. In the traditional ADHD evaluation conducted by the psychiatrist, Lawrence's mother was asked to fill out a Connors Rating Scale. Evidently his Connors score was high, indicating a diagnosis of ADHD.

Exhibit 3.1. SMART Teacher Rating Scale.

Child's Name: _____

Gender: M F

Birthdate: _____ / _____ / _____
Month   Day   Year

Age: _____   School Grade: _____

Teacher's Name: _____

Today's Date: _____

Instructions: Below are a number of common skills that help children succeed in school. Please rate each item according to the student's behavior in the last month. For each item, ask yourself, "How much does this apply to the child?" and circle the best answer for each one. If none, not at all, seldom, or very infrequently, you would circle 0. If very much true or if it occurs very often or frequently, you would circle 3. You would circle 1 or 2 for ratings in between. Please respond to each item.

	NOT TRUE AT ALL	JUST A LITTLE TRUE	PRETTY MUCH TRUE	VERY MUCH TRUE
1. Attentive, able to focus	0	1	2	3
2. Cooperates with my instructions	0	1	2	3
3. Able to sit still when given a subject he or she is interested in	0	1	2	3
4. Remembers what he/she has already learned	0	1	2	3
5. Able to make and keep friends	0	1	2	3
6. Respectful to adults	0	1	2	3
7. Shows maturity for age	0	1	2	3
8. Good in spelling	0	1	2	3

	0	1	2	3
9. Can remain still	0	1	2	3
10. Tireless, results oriented	0	1	2	3
11. Respects the rights of others	0	1	2	3
12. Is able to harness energy into productive activities such as athletics	0	1	2	3
13. Reading up to par	0	1	2	3
14. Demonstrates ability to learn	0	1	2	3
15. Is artistic	0	1	2	3
16. Pays attention to things he/she is really interested in	0	1	2	3
17. Is effective when given choice to be his or her own boss; is independent	0	1	2	3
18. Shows interest in schoolwork	0	1	2	3
19. Eager to try new things; gets excited	0	1	2	3
20. Controls temper outbursts	0	1	2	3
21. Is creative, curious, intuitive	0	1	2	3
22. Good in arithmetic	0	1	2	3
23. Is results oriented	0	1	2	3
24. Can play or engage in leisure activities quietly	0	1	2	3
25. Willing to take risks	0	1	2	3
26. Does follow through on instructions and finishes schoolwork	0	1	2	3
27. Has special abilities	0	1	2	3
28. Is good at the computer	0	1	2	3

Exhibit 3.2. SMART Parent Rating Scale.

Child's Name: _____

Birthdate: _____ / _____ / _____   Age: _____   School Grade: _____
          Month   Day   Year

Gender:
M F

Parent's Name: _____   Today's Date: _____

Instructions: Below are a number of common skills that help children succeed at home. Please rate each item according to the student's behavior in the last month. For each item, ask yourself, "How much does this apply to my child?" and circle the best answer for each one. If none, not at all, seldom, or very infrequently, you would circle 0. If very much true, or it occurs very often or frequently, you would circle 3. You would circle 1 or 2 for ratings in between. Please respond to each item.

	NOT TRUE AT ALL	JUST A LITTLE TRUE	PRETTY MUCH TRUE	VERY MUCH TRUE
1. Attentive	0	1	2	3
2. Able to control anger	0	1	2	3
3. Can complete homework	0	1	2	3
4. Is tireless	0	1	2	3
5. Maintains attention with things he/she is interested in	0	1	2	3
6. Respectful with adults	0	1	2	3
7. Shows honesty	0	1	2	3
8. Completes chores	0	1	2	3

	0	1	2	3
9. Can control in malls or while grocery shopping	0	1	2	3
10. Gets along with siblings	0	1	2	3
11. Follows house rules	0	1	2	3
12. Shows good appetite	0	1	2	3
13. Feels a part of the family	0	1	2	3
14. Accepts blame for mistakes	0	1	2	3
15. Is creative, has special abilities	0	1	2	3
16. Good at the computer	0	1	2	3
17. Tolerates criticism well	0	1	2	3
18. Able to think before acting	0	1	2	3
19. Can focus on more than one thing at a time	0	1	2	3
20. Sleeps OK for age	0	1	2	3
21. Demonstrates a sense of fair play	0	1	2	3
22. Can wait in lines or await turn in games or group situations	0	1	2	3
23. Is physically healthy	0	1	2	3
24. Gets up in the morning OK	0	1	2	3
25. Accepts compliments well	0	1	2	3
26. Is curious, likes to learn	0	1	2	3
27. Is good with his/her hands	0	1	2	3

In my first meeting with Lawrence and his mother, I asked him what he was good at. Lawrence was unable to think of any abilities or qualities that were separate from ADHD. To help identify strengths, I then asked his mother to fill out my SMART scale. To Lawrence's surprise, his mother rated him as 2 or 3 on fifteen of the twenty-seven skills. His best skills, according to his mother, were "good at the computer" and "is curious, likes to learn." I then used these abilities in therapy to help Lawrence build a more competency-based story about himself.

Collaborative Goal Setting

Once I have gathered enough information about the problem and what it means to the family, I begin to identify the strengths of the child. I then invite the family to set initial treatment goals. Goal setting is critical to the therapeutic outcome. This process helps the therapy move from problem talk to solution talk. As a lead-in to this discussion, I might share with the family the following: "Now let's talk about what you want to be different—where you want to be if therapy is successful." Goals need to be well formulated and specific so as to increase the possibility of achieving therapeutic success (Walter and Peller, 1992). Getting specific helps me see whether the goals are realistic, and later, whether they have been met. Through a collaborative inquiry, the family and I create a focus for therapy. Well-formed treatment goals are

- Salient to the family (the family's goal, not the therapist's)
- Small
- Concrete, specific, and behavioral
- The presence rather than the absence of something
- A beginning rather than an end
- Realistic and achievable within the child's and family's life

Here are some examples of goal-setting questions I might ask in a first interview:

> Suppose you go to bed tonight, and while you are sleeping a miracle happens and ADHD is gone. When you wake up the next day, how will you be able to tell that your miracle really happened? What will be different?
>
> Who will be most surprised—your [mother, father, or sibling] when you do that?
>
> How about school? What will be the first thing your teacher notices that indicates that you have changed?
>
> Mom, what will be one small sign that your son is changing?
>
> What will be one small sign that things are heading in a direction that your son will feel a bit more in control of his life?
>
> Which of your child's strengths, as identified in the SMART scale, will be most likely to help him change?
>
> How will you know when therapy has ended? What will your son be doing differently that tells you we no longer need to meet?

Here's an example of goal setting from my own experience: Brett, eleven years old and living with his mother, a single parent, was diagnosed ADHD, inattentive type, by his pediatrician. He was having problems completing his homework; he became distracted by video games or television. Although he was very bright, Brett's grades had nose-dived to a D average. When I asked the goal questions, Brett and his mother came up with three goals. Brett would (1) initiate his own homework without request from his mother, (2) complete his homework in a quiet room without the TV on, and (3) improve his grades to a B average by the end of the semester.

The Medication Option

Postmodern therapies are sometimes misrepresented by traditional clinicians as approaches that reject all notions of biological influence in the life of problems such as ADHD. On the contrary, a postmodern or SMART therapist is concerned with the privileging of biological explanations over other constructions, particularly contextual, societal, gender, and cultural factors. I tell parents that their ADHD child does not have a biological defect but a biological difference that has challenges to it (sitting still in a classroom) and strengths (being tireless, energetic, creative).

The issue of stimulant medication often comes up during the intake assessment. Either the child is already taking medication or the parents are seriously considering putting their child on it (and want a referral to our child psychiatrist). I clearly state my concerns about the effects of Ritalin. Often the parents have not received this information and are grateful. Others prefer to have their child see the child psychiatrist for a medication evaluation. Because I am not a physician, I do not make the decision for them; under certain circumstances, I refer the child to a psychiatric colleague in my clinic.

I am more likely to refer for medication if the following criteria are met (Nylund and Corsiglia, 1996):

- The family has a good understanding of Ritalin, particularly its side effects. I discuss Ritalin's limitations to counter many parents' idea that the medication will solve everything.
- The outcome measures for what the medication may accomplish are co-constructed by the family, the child, and the doctor.
- The family is in control of when and if a trial of medication is started. Parents or children who do not choose the medication option should be complimented and not seen as resistant to treatment.

- The psychiatrist uses common everyday language with the child.
- The child's concerns about the medication are taken into account, explored, and destigmatized.
- Possible side effects of the medication are constantly and vigilantly monitored.
- The parents and the child can choose when and whether to take the child off the medication.

I am especially interested in the message the child receives about taking medication. If the message is that taking Ritalin is proof that he or she is crazy, defective, or diseased, I like to ask the parent these questions (Nylund and Corsiglia, 1994):

What message(s) do you think your child is receiving about having to take Ritalin?

Would it concern you if your child gets the message that he or she is damaged due to taking Ritalin?

How can you monitor the possible side effects of the medication?

What might be a useful way of telling your child why he or she has to take Ritalin?

These questions can help parents develop a critical lens through which to view medication treatment and can help parents de-pathologize their child.

A Word of Caution

Having conducted the assessment, I move the treatment ahead to the first step in the SMART approach. We are ready to get back in Huck's raft to move toward solutions. But let's be careful. This five-step SMART approach is meant only as a guide to working with

ADHD children. The five steps follow the practices of narrative therapy (White and Epston, 1990). I use the acronym SMART to assist and guide therapists in their use of therapeutic questions; many therapists I supervise find the acronym helpful when learning the steps of narrative therapy. Although this approach is effective, I don't recommend rigid adherence to it. Therapy usually does not progress along a straight line; typically there are ups and downs.

Therapeutic conversations can sometimes be messy, so when it comes to the application of these steps in practice, it may be more useful to think in terms of cyclical progression rather than linear progression. I may find myself cycling around the steps many times during a therapy relationship and even in one session. But for the sake of learning the techniques so you can use them whenever appropriate, let's next row ahead to the first step—separating the problem from the child.

Chapter Four

Step One

Separating the Problem of ADHD
from the Child

In *The Adventures of Huckleberry Finn*, the Widow Douglas refers to Huck as a poor lost lamb. Certainly, parents, teachers, and friends of children labeled ADHD have developed a host of adjectives to describe their behaviors, including hyper, defiant, out of control, spacey, distracted, and disordered.

Michael White and David Epston (1990) refer to these types of descriptions as "internalizing discourses" (p. 10). Internalizing discourses constitute the dominant, psychiatric way of speaking about therapy clients. Although clinicians may not use colloquial insults, the language of the DSM-IV and various psychological theories can be experienced as a sophisticated form of name calling. Typically, internalizing discourses are deficit-saturated, pathological labels that locate the problem within the client's biology or identity. These labels become "totalizing" descriptions of the client, leaving out other important aspects of the client's identity such as his skill, at times, in managing the problem successfully.

The ADHD label is a powerful example of an internalizing description. Children who exhibit ADHD symptoms in one context are often referred to as ADHD, as if they have *become* the disorder. Evidence of the child's ability to defeat the problem in other contexts is often ignored. Furthermore, people begin to filter all of their experiences with the child through the lens of ADHD. All behaviors, regular and irregular, are attributed to the disorder, often at the expense of the child's creativity and ability to cope.

To counter the negative effects of internalizing labels, White and Epston (1990) developed a therapeutic practice called *externalizing the problem*—a term that refers to the therapeutic practice of naming the problem and linguistically separating it from the child. This practice of separating the problem from the child is the first step in the SMART therapy approach.

Narrative therapists view these externalizing conversations as powerful tools to help children realize that they are more than the sum of their ADHD symptoms. Externalizing conversations create distance between the child's identity and the problem, making space for the child to consider who and how he would like to be by identifying skills, resources, and preferences.

Some critics have referred to these conversations as simple cheerleading or as a way to minimize the effects of problems in children's lives. But White, Epston, and their colleagues look at it as a philosophical and political practice designed to reverse the ever-increasing trend toward pathologizing and objectifying persons according to dominant cultural specifications (such as the DSM-IV). White and Epston (1990) state that the externalizing process is helpful because it reduces unproductive conflict over who is accountable for the problem. In addition, externalizing the problem helps people cooperate and work against the problem rather than each other. And last, separating the problem allows people to take a more playful and less serious approach to solving problems.

- It decreases conflict over who is responsible for the problem.
- It reduces the sense of failure people have in response to not having solved the problem.
- It unites people against the problem rather than against each other.
- It opens the way for people to reclaim their lives from problems.
- It liberates people to view the problem in new ways (Parry and Doan, 1994, p. 53).

Externalizing conversations develop fluid descriptions of clients, their lives, and their problems. In externalizing conversations, we pay attention to how the client's relationship with the problem evolved over time. This takes the pressure off the therapist to come up with a succinct and tidy externalization that will remain static and constant throughout the therapy. Instead, this more fluid description acknowledges that conversations, like problems and solutions, have their twists and turns. In addition, externalizing conversations acknowledge that clients are often influenced by simultaneous and multiple problems that become entangled.

I have found the practice of externalizing to be extremely valuable in my work with children labeled ADHD. By naming and separating the problem of ADHD from the child, I am aligned on the same side of the problem as the child. The child becomes the expert about the problem, and I become a curious investigator. The medicalized and deficit description of ADHD begins to lose its weight, as the child, family, and I work together to undermine its influence.

This chapter describes the first step in the SMART process: separating (or externalizing) the problem of ADHD from the child. I offer practical suggestions for developing externalizing conversation with children and families. In addition, I list some examples of externalizing questions and illustrate some ways to separate the problem through case examples and transcripts. Pick up your oars! Let's go!

Externalizing ADHD

During the first therapy session I typically interview one or both parents, along with the child. After conducting the SMART assessment, I listen carefully to the child's and the family's concerns. In the beginning of the interview, I establish rapport with family, which includes the basic therapeutic skills of attending, paraphrasing, clarifying, and summarizing. As in any therapy, there is always a process of selecting what gets ignored and what gets attended to. I respectfully listen to the problem story but remain attentive for indications of the child's competencies. I also avoid using internalizing and totalizing language about the problem.

Right from the beginning, I separate the problem from the child in my mind as I listen and respond. I do this by creating a competency-focused conversation in which the child is separate from the problem. That takes practice. For example, if the parent describes Jane as ADHD, I might respond by saying, "So, Jane is influenced by ADHD?" This type of reply begins the process of externalizing conversations. Another strategy I use is to ask questions such as "How does ADHD influence your child?" and "How does ADHD influence your household?" These types of questions linguistically suggest that ADHD is something *outside* the child's own identity.

Naming the Problem

After I have listened intently and with obvious curiosity, I invite the child and family to name the problem. I encourage them to describe the problem in a way that is close to the child's language, voice, and experience. By naming the problem in the child's terms, I learn much more about the child's view of the problem than whatever the typical, clinical name would suggest. Some examples of the descriptions that children have come up with include the Hyper Monster, Fidgetiness, Distraction, and the Hurricane. Teens tend to prefer calling the problem by its clinical name, ADHD.

Here are some recommendations for engaging children and families in externalizing conversations:

- Don't rush to externalize the first thing the parent or child talks about. Listen carefully to a thorough explication of the problem to make sure the externalized description captures the breadth and complexity of the problem (Winslade and Monk, 1999).

- Think of ADHD (and its associated symptoms) as a thing, object, or person; talk about it as an active agent in the child's and family's life (Zimmerman and Dickerson, 1996).
- Encourage the child to create a name for the problem.
- If the child or parent cannot think of a name, tentatively suggest one and come to some agreement about using it. It helps to recall names that other clients have used rather than rely on one that comes from a clinician.
- It is OK to refer to the problem as "the problem" or "it" or "ADHD" in the beginning. As time goes by, a clearer description will materialize. While waiting for this to happen, continue to explore the general themes in the child's life without honing in too narrowly on finding one name for the problem.
- It is often helpful to be explicit with families and tell them that you are externalizing the problem.

Asking Questions

Here are some examples of questions that I might use in the beginning of the externalizing process:

ADHD is the doctor's name for the problem. What name would you give it?

Families have found it helpful to view the problem as something outside the child. It helps to bring some new ideas on the problem and can pave the way for solutions. Is it OK if we experiment with talking about ADHD in this way?

So, has ADHD been running the show? Since when? How much of the time?

When did ADHD show up in your life?

What part of your body does ADHD show up in first?

Would you like to call the problem ADHD or some other name?

These are just a few examples of questions a SMART therapist might ask in a first session. I offer them only as a guide, not as an inflexible, predetermined template. Instead of entering the first session with some rehearsed questions, I prefer to ask questions that come out of an evolving conversation with the child and family. I find that clients often come up with delightful, rich, and creative names for problems that tell me much more about how the problem is affecting them than more traditional labels would. Now let's turn to some case examples that depict the practice of separating the problem. The following example illustrates the practice of introducing externalizing conversations in a first interview.

Case Example: The Girl Who Had the Tickles

Nicole, a very talented and quick-witted eight-year-old, came up with her own unique name for ADHD. Nicole was referred to me because of her teacher's concern that she might be ADHD. Both of her parents attended the initial interview. According to the school reports, Nicole was having difficulty with attention and hyperactivity. The teacher had recommended a medication evaluation. After conducting the SMART assessment, I asked the following questions to separate the problem from Nicole. Here's a portion of the transcript (Nylund and Corsiglia, 1996):

> *David:* What's your understanding of ADHD?
>
> *Mom:* Well, I think it has to do with problems paying attention.
>
> *David:* So that's what you have heard from the teacher?
>
> *Mom:* Yes, she seems real concerned and thinks Nicole needs Ritalin. We're concerned, too.
>
> *David:* How have you expressed your concerns to Nicole? Have you talked with her about it?
>
> *Mom:* Yes, Nicole said it's hard to listen to the teacher and sit still.
>
> *David:* Is it tough sometimes, Nicole, to listen to the teacher?

Nicole: Yes.

David: Do you have fun with your energy? What kinds of
     things do you do with your energy?

Nicole: I like to play outside.

Mom: She's good at soccer and other sports.

David: Really! So using her energy is one of her best talents?

Dad: Yes, she can be a lot of fun. She's very social.

David: Does your energy, Nicole, make it tough sometimes to
     listen to the teacher?

Nicole: Yes.

[later in the session]

David: Is school fun or boring to you?

Nicole: Boring. . . . My mind wanders.

David: Your teacher wonders if that is ADHD. You know,
     when it's hard to sit still and listen to the teacher. . . .
     What would you call it?

Nicole: [Ponders] Tickles.

David: Tickles! That's a great name! [family laughs] So what
     do the Tickles get you to do?

Nicole: They make my feet tired because I go like this
     [demonstrates by swinging her legs back and forth].
     My hands hurt too after awhile, because I move them
     around, too.

David: What else do the Tickles do?

Nicole: I can't sit still in my chair.

David: Do the Tickles lead to trouble?

Nicole: Sometimes the teacher has to remind me to get back
     in my seat [pp. 172–173].

In this example, I began the interview by exploring the family's
meaning of ADHD. I also invited Nicole and her parents to discuss
her abilities and talents (soccer and sports). I made a mental note
of these abilities and used them later on in therapy (step 4—
reclaiming special abilities). Last, I invited Nicole to name the

problem that is influencing her. She creatively named the problem Tickles. After naming and separating the problem from Nicole's identity, I then moved into discussing the effects of the Tickles in her life. This is step 2 of the SMART approach (mapping the effects of ADHD on the child and family), which will be discussed at length in Chapter Five.

Interviewing ADHD

One of the ways I introduce externalizing conversations to children with ADHD and their parents is through an exercise developed by Sallyann Roth and David Epston (1996, p. 148) that they call "consulting the problem." In this exercise, I role play ADHD while a colleague role plays an investigative reporter who is writing an exposé on the problem. This exercise is conducted in the presence of the family. By role playing ADHD, the problem becomes further personified and separated from the child.

There are three parts to the exercise. In the first part, my colleague (who is playing the investigative reporter) interviews me (as ADHD) on the ways ADHD achieves influence over the child and family. The questions the reporters asks attempt to expose

- ADHD's purposes
- ADHD's goals for the child's life
- The innumerable techniques ADHD uses to get its way
- Who stands with ADHD, that is, what people and forces are in league with it

In the second part, the reporter interviews ADHD about when it has failed—occasions when ADHD has had little or no influence on the child. This part of the interview is based on the premise that ADHD is never totally successful in its ambitions for a child's or for the family's life. The reporter asks about the following:

- Times when the child has frustrated ADHD's plans and goals
- What the child has done to keep some territory safe from ADHD's grasp
- The goals of the child
- Who stands with the child (parents, relatives, friends, teachers, therapists, and so on)

In the third part of the interview, the child and family are asked about their experience of the exercise. They have the opportunity to comment on the accuracy of the portrayal of the problem. The child and the parents are asked to share their thoughts on proposals for action that might further undermine the influence of ADHD in the child's life.

Families find this exercise to be fun and helpful. After the exercises, clients begin to conceptualize ADHD as external to the child.

The following is a case example in which I used this exercise with Nick, an eleven-year-old boy, and his mother, Janet, who was a single parent.

Case Example: Nick's Math Talent

Nick was referred to me after being diagnosed ADHD, hyperactive-impulsive type, by his pediatrician. Nick was having problems controlling his anger; he was fidgeting in his seat at school and talking excessively in class. His doctor thought therapy might help Nick improve his ability to control his impulses. He was also placed on Ritalin for his hyperactivity.

In the second session, I saw Nick and Janet in my clinic's reflecting team time. Reflecting teams (Andersen, 1991; White, 1991)—a format in which colleagues observe the session behind a one-way mirror and then comment on the session while the family watches—are valuable in highlighting the new story. As we began to engage in an externalizing conversation about ADHD, I thought it might be useful to conduct the consulting-the-problem exercise. Nick was really playful and creative, and I thought the exercise would help further separate the problem from him. In addition, Nick had made some improvements between the first and second session; the exercise might be a way to highlight those accomplishments.

I asked a colleague, Tom, to join me in front of the mirror with the family and become an investigative reporter. I took on the role of ADHD. Here's an excerpt from that interview:

> *Tom (as the reporter):* So, ADHD, what are you doing to Nick?
>
> *ADHD (Dave):* I take over his mind and body and get him to not pay attention in class and squirm in his seat.
>
> *Tom:* Do you do anything else to him?
>
> *ADHD:* Of course! Many things if you don't mind me being a bit of a braggart about my success with Nick! I team up with my friend, Temper, and get him to have angry outbursts in class. I get him to be a slave to his moods. I also get him to forget to do his homework. This leads to battles at home with his mother about his schoolwork.
>
> *Tom:* So, ADHD, do you work on Mom too?
>
> *ADHD:* Why yes! I take advantage of mother-blaming and exploit Janet's guilt. I get her to think she's responsible for his homework and she's a bad parent if he does poorly in school. I put an idea in her head that, because Nick is ADHD, he can't be responsible for his own actions and his own homework . . . that he is an incapable and damaged person.
>
> *Tom:* So, is mother-blaming one of your best friends?
>
> *ADHD:* Definitely! I love to exploit single-parent mothers who have challenging and spirited children. Mothers are told

in our culture that their identity as a parent is reflected in their child's behavior. With children who are energetic and challenging, I become really popular with mothers. They no longer have to blame themselves. Their child's behavior is due to a medical condition. This gets moms off the hook.

Tom: What else has made you so popular?

ADHD: [Squirms] Pharmaceutical companies. They and many other people profit from my being so widely diagnosed. I have made them very rich! Most parents don't know that the United States consumes 90 percent of the total amount of Ritalin in the world.

Tom: What are some of your other friends?

ADHD: The belief in a 100 percent biological basis of behavior. I am very popular because we tend to give a biological explanation for kids' behaviors. Little do most parents know, however, that there is no evidence that I am a discrete, biological entity.

Tom: Man! You have many friends! Any others?

ADHD: Why yes! A short attention span, so common in our culture. With our rapid-fire culture here in the United States, kids have a hard time coping with slowness. With fax machines, fast-paced TV shows, video games, kids have a need for speed. This makes it hard for kids like Nick to sit still in a classroom and pace themselves, particularly if there's a boring teacher who doesn't know how to handle a big class full of unruly kids.

Tom: What's your goal in Nick's life?

ADHD: Ultimately, I want him to believe he has to settle for less in life because of his ADHD and drop out of school. I want him to break the rules in school . . . to get into more fights . . . develop a reputation as a troublemaker. I also want him and his mother to forget about his talents and become passive onlookers while I run the show . . . to feel helpless before me. I want them to believe that medication is the only solution . . . that they have to rely on the experts. I want them to ignore their own knowledge in solving their problems.

Tom: Wow! It sounds like you have a well-formulated plan for Nick's life. But it sounds dismal. Have you been completely successful? Have you convinced Nick and Janet that there is nothing they can do about you?

ADHD: Well, I hate to be honest . . . but . . . OK, I have to admit that Nick and Janet are trying to make a comeback.

Tom: Oh yeah? How so?

ADHD: This past week, Nick started doing his homework without having been reminded. And he had no temper out-bursts at home or school. Also, his therapist found out today that he is a whiz at math!

Tom: Why were you upset when David found out that Nick has a talent in math?

ADHD: Because it's getting Nick to think he is smart and capable. I don't like that. I would rather he think he is dumb!

Tom: What do you think about Nick having no temper this week?

ADHD: It makes me want to have a tantrum!

Tom: What do you think these steps mean for you?

ADHD: Well, if he kept it up, I might not be so powerful in his life.

Tom: What do you think it says about Nick that he has made a comeback? What is Nick like apart from you?

ADHD: Well, he is creative and bright and he has ability. I have some respect for Nick, but don't let him know that!

[later in the exercise]

David (no longer as ADHD): What did you think of the exercise Nick?

Nick: I thought it was funny.

David: Does it make you want to do anything with ADHD?

Nick: Yeah, I want to get rid of it.

David: You do? How about you Janet? What was this exercise like for you?

Janet: [Laughing] Well, it made me think about some new ideas about ADHD.

David: What new ideas?

Janet: Well, I hadn't really thought about why ADHD is so popular. Nor had I thought so much about what the label could do to him. I plan to work hard at noticing his talents.

The interview ended soon after the role play. It appeared the consulting-the-problem exercise was helpful in deconstructing some of the ideas about ADHD that the family had taken for granted. Janet gained some new perspectives on ADHD that enabled her to notice Nick's abilities. The exercise also seemed to punctuate some of the recent positive steps Nick was taking to undermine the influence of ADHD. Role playing ADHD set the stage for a strength-based therapy.

Expressive Arts Therapy

Conventional treatment approaches for ADHD rely on "talking" therapy and focus primarily on working with parents to develop behavior-control strategies. In addition to working with parents, the SMART approach enters children's worlds. Some children I see can engage actively in verbal conversation. Most, however, prefer to express themselves in ways other than sitting and talking.

I have found that children labeled ADHD are highly creative and are excited to communicate in artistic ways such as using puppets, drawings, or computer graphics. If children are not provided with alternative means of expression, they can be excluded or marginalized in the therapeutic process. These more artistic ways of intervening are referred to as a "playful approach to serious problems" (Freeman, Epston, and Lobovits, 1997, p. 3).

I use expressive arts therapy under the following circumstances:

- With children who are not very verbal, including those who have language-based difficulties or are too young to speak

- With children for whom art, sand tray, or drama therapy are their preferred means of communicating

- With children who are primarily visual or kinesthetic processors (such as many kids labeled ADHD)

- With children who find communicating verbally about the problem uncomfortable and find expressive arts less threatening

Expressive arts therapy is congruent with the practice of externalizing. The very process of drawing or dramatizing the problem naturally evokes a visceral sense of the problem as separate from the child. By drawing the problem, the child can see it more clearly and ponder it more easily. These more artistic ways of expressing themselves tend to bring forth creative and imaginative solutions.

The SMART approach employs expressive arts techniques. However, because SMART therapists are not using the art in traditional ways, the approach does not require any special training in traditional expressive arts therapy. Typically, I invite children to draw the problem of ADHD and then draw a counter-problem picture in which the child is in charge of ADHD. I am not the expert interpreting the "true" meaning of the picture. Instead, my stance of curiosity facilitates the expansion of the child's preferred meanings. The artwork becomes a tool to highlight a new story for the child, who is the expert and whose meanings are privileged. Thus, expressive arts therapy is not employed for so-called objective diagnostic and interpretive purposes. Here are a few case examples.

Case Example: Vic the Astronomer

Vic, age thirteen, came in with a diagnosis of ADHD, inattentive type. He was doing poorly in school, especially in terms of his grades, because he had difficulty doing his homework. His teacher and parents were frustrated with him because he had ability—he just wasn't putting it into practice. His parents were concerned that his poor grades would keep him out of college and destroy Vic's dream of being an astronomer. On his SMART rating scale, he scored very high on "good at computers."

I decided to use his computer skill by having him make a computer image of what ADHD looks like when it has the upper hand. I also asked him to make a computer image of what it looks like when Vic has the upper hand. Last, I invited him to make a third computer image: what his future will look like when ADHD is in the "back seat of his life."

Vic brought three imaginative computer images to the next session. In the first graphic (Figure 4.1) he depicts how ADHD makes homework a burden for him. The second (Figure 4.2) depicts Vic getting the upper hand on ADHD and graduating from high school. Vic shows himself as an astronomer in the third graphic (Figure 4.3).

These graphics helped Vic generate creativity and motivation to improve his concentration and do his homework.

Figure 4.1. Young Boy.

Figure 4.2. Young Boy.

Figure 4.3. Look Like a Scientist.

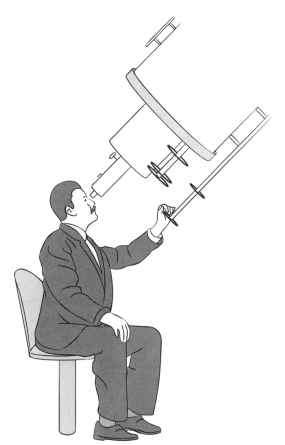

Case Example: Scott and the Hurricane

Scott, age ten and diagnosed ADHD, hyperactive type, had a very difficult time sitting still in my office. He hopped from chair to chair, swinging his arms and legs; he talked nonstop and turned my light switch on and off. He would only sit still if he was involved in some art project, according to his mother. I decided to use his artistic abilities by asking him to draw what ADHD looks like to him. He thought about it for awhile and then drew a hurricane and labeled it "F-5." I asked him about the drawing and he said, "My ADHD makes me act like a hurricane . . . a big one, the size of an F-5" (the measurement assigned to a large hurricane). I then asked him if he could calm his hurricane, and he said yes. Next, I asked him what size he could make it. He said, "An F–2." He then drew an F-2 (smaller) hurricane.

Future sessions focused on ways he could calm his hurricane to an F-2. The drawings helped personify the problem and gave Scott a visceral and tangible technique to slow himself down. His teacher and mother noticed a significant improvement after the pictures were drawn.

This chapter described step 1 in our SMART program: the practice of separating or externalizing the problem of ADHD from the child. In contrast to traditional descriptions of ADHD, separating the problem from the child means the child's identity is spared the deficit-saturated, pathological label. By separating the problem from the child, space is opened for other kinds of conversations that promote creativity, strengths, and strategies.

Once ADHD is externalized, questions can be asked to determine the influence of ADHD in the child's life—the focus of the next chapter. Let's plunge ahead.

Chapter Five

Step Two

Mapping the Influence of ADHD on the Child and Family

Once the problem of ADHD is named and separated from the child, the SMART therapist works with the family to develop an understanding of the myriad effects of the problem on the child and on the family's life. This process is called mapping the influence of the problem; it invites the child and family to make a detailed account of the often tyrannizing influence of ADHD in their lives.

Many therapies encourage clients to examine their problems. In traditional therapies, however, problems are typically seen as "belonging" to the client and representing some kind of deficit or character flaw. To a certain extent, the client must admit ownership of the problem in order begin the healing process. Clients who fail to admit their ownership are considered to be in denial.

For instance, were Huckleberry Finn and the Widow Douglas to enter traditional therapy, Huckleberry's "biological condition" (ADHD) would be the central focus of conversation. Huckleberry would take Ritalin and perhaps be assigned to a social skills group to learn to manage his disorder. The Widow Douglas would learn to focus on the symptoms of Huckleberry's disorder as she dutifully reported his progress (or lack thereof) to the psychiatrist in medication management meetings. In therapy or at CHADD meetings the Widow Douglas would also receive encouragement to examine certain deficits in her parenting and would be taught to more consistently deploy cognitive-behavioral parenting strategies. If she didn't follow through with the parenting strategies, she might be viewed by the traditional clinician as resistant or in denial.

In contrast, SMART therapy places the problem outside the client. If Huckleberry and the Widow Douglas were to enter SMART therapy, they would be encouraged to think about ADHD and their resources to resist it in markedly different ways. As we saw in Chapter Four, in SMART therapy the problem is often referred to as an independent, mischievous entity with designs on the child and family's happiness. From this externalized position, the child and family are free to account for the devastating influence of the problem without viewing themselves from a deficit-saturated position.

Mapping the influence of the problem is a critical step in SMART therapy because it allows the therapist to enter the world of the child and family and to learn the specific ways ADHD may be wreaking havoc. SMART therapists do not rely solely on the DSM-IV to understand what ADHD can do to a child. SMART therapists do not assume they know all of ADHD's plans and tactics for ruining a family's life. Instead, we trust our expert guides— the clients—to instruct us regarding ADHD's particular strategies. Consequently, Huckleberry and the Widow Douglas would be encouraged to make a detailed account of ADHD's impact on their lives. This account may include ADHD's problematic influence on their relationship, its effects on Huckleberry's academic and social life, its influence on the Widow Douglas, and the reputation it is building for Huck and his family.

This is a crucial step in SMART therapy—exploring the problematic effects of ADHD with the family. In this process the child's and family's meanings are privileged over expert meanings. The child is able to give a very precise and vivid account of ADHD's effects on him and others around him.

SMART therapists ask two kinds of questions to map the influence of the problem: (1) "effects" questions and (2) "deconstruction" questions. Effects questions are derived from Michael White's (1989) ideas about relative influence questioning. He writes:

> Relative influence questioning invites family members to derive two
> different descriptions of their association with the problem that they

present for therapy. The first is a description of the influences of the problem in the lives and relationships of family members; the second is a description of the influence of family members and their relationships in the life of the problem. Relative influence questioning also invites family members to participate in the construction of a new description of the problem itself—an externalized description [p. 3].

Thus, effects questions enrich and amplify the externalizing process.

Deconstructing questions assist people in unpacking their ideas about ADHD and viewing them from different perspectives (Freedman and Combs, 1996). These questions invite families to locate the problem of ADHD in a wider historical and cultural context.

By way of illustration, a SMART therapist would attempt to help Huck and his caregiver account for the many and various supports for ADHD-like behavior that do not derive solely from Huckleberry's biology. The therapist might ask Huck Finn and the Widow Douglas to consider the effects of race, class, and social context on the family's and community's expectations of him. Further, the therapist might challenge the Widow Douglas and Huck to consider whether alcohol misuse and physical abuse, imposed by Huckleberry's father, had an impact on Huck's developing ideas about the world and his place in it. The therapist would ask the family if Huckleberry's preferences for action and adventure made sense in the context of the time and conditions in which Huck lived. The therapist would then contrast Huckleberry's preferences to the rigid expectations (such as politeness, school attendance, appearance, and prohibition against association with blacks) that were imposed on white boys in the South at that time.

The SMART therapist explores how the culture may contribute and give support to the problem of ADHD. In the next section I offer examples of questions, along with case transcripts, that demonstrate the process of mapping the influence of the problem. Let's examine some effects questions first.

Effects Questions

After the child and I have named the problem, I ask a series of effects questions to determine the history, breadth, and depth of the problem's influence. I also examine the effects of ADHD on all areas of the child's life: school, home, relationships, self-concept, and career plans. Often children and parents have not realized the magnitude of ADHD's effects on them. By showing the impact of ADHD in their lives and relationships, the real effects of the problem are exposed. This revelation can put the problem of ADHD into a different light, challenging the idea that the problem is primarily generated by the child's biology (Freedman and Combs, 1996). Often, "effects" questions overlap with externalizing questions. Here are some examples:

Questions for the Child

What effect does ADHD have on you at school? How does it interfere with your schooling?

What classroom behaviors does ADHD recruit you into?

What does ADHD want you to think about school? How does it want you to act?

What is ADHD's purpose in doing this to you at school?

What does ADHD want you to learn? Is there anything you'd like to be learning instead?

Does ADHD show up during recess? Does it get in the way of your friendships?

Does ADHD follow you home? Has ADHD earned you a reputation at school with the principal or your teacher?

How does ADHD convince you that you can't do anything about it?

Who are ADHD's friends? Is Temper or Boredom a friend of ADHD?

Does Ritalin help you (or not) in your battle against ADHD?

What does ADHD get you to think about yourself?

Does ADHD make you allergic to homework?

How has ADHD affected your parents? In what ways has it made them think you can't do your homework? Does it make them think they are bad parents?

How much of the time is ADHD in charge of you?

When does ADHD seem to have the easiest time getting to you?

When does ADHD have a really hard time getting to you?

Questions for the Parents

What effect has ADHD had on you as his parents? What effect does it have on the family?

Does ADHD get you working harder than your son at his chores?

What does ADHD do to your identity as parents?

When and where do you think ADHD attacks your child?

Does ADHD make you feel helpless and frustrated? When frustration takes over, what kinds of things do you do in relation to your child?

Now let's turn to some case examples that depict the process of asking effects questions.

Case Example: ADD's Effects on Johnny and His Family

The following vignette is a case that family therapist, Matthew Selekman (1997), worked with. Johnny, age ten, was school-referred to Mr. Selekman for ADD (ADHD). He was quite disruptive in class and at home. His mother, Barbara, was remarried and had three other children from her second marriage. Barbara and her husband, Warren (and stepfather to Johnny), described Johnny's

ADD as chronic. Both parents were pessimistic that Johnny could change. Here's a portion of the transcript:

Matthew: How long has ADD been pushing you around?

Barbara: Three years.

Matthew: When ADD is getting the best of Johnny, what sorts of things does it make him do?

Barbara: Well, he is aggravating Ann [seven years old], and he doesn't listen to me. I tell him to put his things away and he tells me to shut up. Boy, does he get a mouth on him!

Matthew: What about you, Warren? Does ADD coach Johnny to push your buttons as well?

Warren: Yes! I always have to scream at him a few times before he does what I want him to do.

Barbara: Yeah, sometimes it is like talking to the wall. The child is taken over by this ADD thing.

Matthew: So ADD brainwashes him to get out of control? Or does it invade his body like an evil spirit?

Barbara: Warren, wouldn't you say it was like an evil spirit?

Warren: Yes. He gets mad and mouthy and very difficult to manage.

Matthew: When ADD is getting the best of your parents, what does it make the two of you do?

Warren: We argue a lot about how to manage him. I think she is too lenient. I'm more the screamer.

Barbara: I don't like it when Warren screams so much. So to try and keep things calm, I let Johnny off the hook. I know it's wrong, but I don't know . . . I feel frustrated.

Matthew: So ADD divides the two of you? Do both of you feel frustrated by what ADD is doing to this family?

Warren: Yes, I feel frustrated too. This ADD thing has made life hell. We can't leave Johnny alone with Ann.

Matthew: Johnny, what does ADD coach you to do in class?

Johnny: I fight. I don't listen to the teacher. I get mad a lot.

Matthew: Does ADD ever make you feel dumb?

Johnny: Yeah [looking sad].

Matthew: What else does ADD try and teach you about yourself?

Johnny: I'm not a good boy. I can't do the work [pp. 85–86].

Case Example: ADHD's Plot Against Brendan

Brendan was a ten-year-old boy I saw, along with his single-parent father, Eric. Eric thought it was a good idea for Brendan to see a therapist after he was diagnosed with ADHD and placed on Ritalin. Brendan was rebellious in class; he was having problems controlling his anger. Eric was concerned about the troublemaker reputation he was developing at school. Here's our discussion on the effects of ADHD (Brendan's father, Jack, was in the room with us, listening to our conversation):

David: What does ADHD mean to you?

Brendan: It means I have hyperactivity. I can't eat sugar or I won't be able to focus.

David: ADHD makes it hard for you to focus?

Brendan: Yeah. It makes me get distracted real easy. It makes me do things I'm not supposed to be doing. Like right now (swinging his legs back and forth).

David: So right now the ADHD is taking charge? [Brendan smiles and nods yes.] What is ADHD doing to your body right now?

Brendan: Making my legs go up and down [laughing].

David: When is the ADHD most likely to show up?

Brendan: During social studies!

David: During social studies. . . . Why in social studies?

Brendan: Because social studies is really boring.

David: Does ADHD have a friend in Boredom?

Brendan: Yes. Boredom makes me all hyper and stuff. Like in social studies. Social studies is the most boring thing in the whole world!

David: So when the Boredom attacks you, what kinds of things does the ADHD get you to do?

Brendan: Swing my legs back and forth. I move my chair all around. I tap my pencil on the desk all day. I talk to other kids when I should be listening to the teacher.

David: So if the ADHD had its way with you, how does it want you to act at school?

Brendan: It wants me to do whatever I feel like doing! Like run around in the classroom and say, "I hate school!"

David: So, does ADHD make you allergic to school?

Brendan: Yeah! It makes me think school stinks! It makes me just want to watch a movie rather than go to boring school!

David: So ADHD would rather have you watch a movie than go to social studies?

Brendan: Yeah!

David: When you are in social studies, what does ADHD do to your brain?

Brendan: It makes my brain crazy. It makes me want to run out of the classroom and make the biggest mess I can!

David: So ADHD has a very good friend in Boredom. Does ADHD have other friends?

Brendan: Oh definitely! Fighting!

David: Fighting? Why Fighting?

Brendan: Well, it's like you're bored and somebody bothers you and you just hit him! And I hit my sister a lot at home. I guess I have a real temper.

David: So Temper is a friend of ADHD? [Brendan nods yes.] Does Temper show up at school?

Brendan: Oh yeah!

David: And what does that lead to?

Brendan: Trouble! [smiling]

David: I'm laughing, so I have to write this down. ADHD has Boredom, Fighting, Temper, Allergy to School, and Trouble as friends. Is that right? [Brendan nods yes.] What does ADHD want you to think of your teacher?

Brendan: It wants me to think that my teacher is stupid. ADHD tells me, "You don't want to listen to her!"

David: I see. ADHD make you not pay attention to your teacher. What does ADHD want you to pay attention to?

Brendan: My friends, Trouble . . . anything but school.

David: Does ADHD make you think anything about yourself?

Brendan: Well yeah. It makes me think I'm stupid. Like I'm trying to do my homework and it's really hard and ADHD tells my mind, "You're dumb, you will never finish it."

David: Does ADHD almost convince you of those lies?

Brendan: Well, not really. It doesn't convince me.

David: No, how come? What do you do to keep ADHD from tricking you into the lie that you are dumb?

Brendan: I just do the work!

David: Wow! I would like to ask more about how you don't listen to ADHD. Can I ask that in awhile? [Brendan nods yes.]

Brendan's acknowledgment that he is able to do the work in spite of ADHD appears to be an exception to the problem's influence on him. This might be an entry point into a new story of Brendan's relationship with ADHD, which might allow us to explore Brendan's skills, talents, and influence over the problem. (The process of building and circulating a new story about the child's relationship with ADHD will be discussed in step 3 and step 4 of the SMART therapy process.)

Brendan: Sure, I can do my work. It's not so hard lately.

David: OK, I will ask about that in a few minutes. Don't make me forget. Or should I tell ADHD not to make me forget? [Brendan laughs.] Brendan, let me ask you one more big question: If ADHD has its way with you, what does it ultimately want from you? What does it want you to end up as?

Brendan: It wants me to be suspended from every school in the world! ADHD wants to be my life . . . to tell me what to do.

David: Wow, ADHD has a very evil plan for you. It doesn't seem to have your best interests at heart, does it?

Brendan: No, it doesn't.

The conversation then turned to (1) what kind of relationship Brendan wanted with ADHD, (2) his future goals and plans, and (3) how to use his talents and "smarts" to trick ADHD. A portion of that discussion is in Chapter Six.

Deconstructing Questions

After asking a series of effects questions, the SMART therapy conversation flows into deconstructing questions. Often the types of questions overlap. Deconstructing questions focus on two areas: (1) the possible negative effects of the ADHD label on children and families and (2) cultural conditions that support and enhance the traditional view of ADHD.

It is important to move slowly and delicately when asking deconstructing questions. As stated previously, many parents are heavily recruited by the conventional discourse. If we move too forcibly and quickly, parents might think we don't understand the severity of the problem.

It has been my experience that after the deconstructive phase, families begin to hold society and the Western educational system accountable for many of the problems associated with ADHD. When the cultural forces that shape the traditional views on ADHD are made visible, parents stop pathologizing their children and begin to notice their talents, skills, and abilities. Parents begin to take up a critical position on the ADHD epidemic. Parents no longer view ADHD as a purely biological problem.

Deconstructing questions also make it possible for young people to feel their own influence over ADHD. Once they have discovered moments when the effects of ADHD didn't seem so strong, they can appreciate their talents and gifts. ADHD no longer speaks to the "truth" of their identity at this point. Here are some useful questions to engage families in the process of deconstruction:

Questions for the Child

Johnny, do you think ADHD is a friend or enemy to you?

Does ADHD try to convince you that you have to settle for less in life?

Why do you think there are so many boys in your class taking Ritalin?

What do you think of your school?

Does school feed Boredom?

What kind of teacher would make ADHD go away? What kind of teacher supports Boredom?

Questions for the Parents

Are you familiar with the idea that kids who have been diagnosed with ADHD are somehow broken or flawed? What effect could that idea have on a child?

Are you familiar with the idea that ADHD is a chemical imbalance? What effect might that have on your child if he felt he had a chemical imbalance? What if you were to view the problem as a living imbalance instead of a chemical imbalance?

How has the way the doctor labeled your son influenced the life of ADHD?

How does the ADHD label affect your son's view of himself?

What options would not be available to you or your child if you accepted the idea that children labeled ADHD must settle for less in life? (Stewart and Nodrick, 1990).

Do you think our schools are set up to meet the unique needs of children? Or does your son's school favor students who sit still and perform repetitive tasks?

What learning styles do you think are most honored in our schools? Does your son's teacher make use of his creative learning style? If she did so, what effect do you think it would have on ADHD?

Should children who learn in different and creative ways be labeled with a deficit?

Do you think ADHD's recent popularity has something to do with more refined clinical measurements? Or does it have to do with other influences such as school overcrowding?

What do you make of the fact that 90 percent of the Ritalin in the world is used in the United States? (DeGrandpre, 1999).

Case Example: Paul Sheds the ADHD Label

The following case example is from narrative therapist Ian Law (1997). It is an interview with Paul, a fourteen-year-old who was diagnosed with ADHD, hyperactive-impulsive type. Paul's problem behaviors included aggression (fighting at school), defiance at school, and hyperactivity. He had been taking Ritalin for awhile but stopped taking it, as the interview shows. Paul lived with his single-parent mother. Paul's father (who was out of the picture at the time of this interview) had subjected Paul and his mother to severe violence in the past.

Here's a segment of Ian and Paul's session:

Ian: Is it right that you have a lot of involvement with doctors and pediatricians?

Paul: What's a pediatrician?

Ian: A pediatrician is a doctor who specializes in seeing young people and children.

Paul: Like Dr. B?

Ian: Is Dr. B a pediatrician?

Paul: I don't know. He's the one that described me as ADHD and all that.

Ian: Right.

Paul: I'm off the medication now, and you know how Mum [lives in Australia] said that I'm not allowed to have Coke and all that because I'm hyperactive.

Ian: Yes.

Paul: I've been having Coke and all, and I'm not hyperactive.

Ian: So can I talk to you about all that?

Paul: About what?

Ian: About being ADHD and hyperactive. When did you first hear about these things?

Paul: About eighteen months ago my mum took me to see Dr. B, and within a few minutes he said I probably have ADHD; I ended up going on medication.

Ian: So around about a year and half ago you went to see this doctor, and he said you had ADHD. Had you ever heard of it before?

Paul: Yeah, I knew a little of it before.

Ian: And what did you understand about it?

Paul: Nothing.

Ian: Do you know what it stands for?

Paul: Attention deficit disorder. But I didn't know it then.

Ian: So what do you understand about it now?

Paul: Well, it's a chemical imbalance in the brain. It's the liquid in your brain that's not equal.

Ian: And what does that chemical imbalance mean? What happens?

Paul: They find it hard to learn, get along with other kids, self-esteem, all that sort of stuff. That's what I think it is.

Ian: So did you know all that time, or is that what you have learned since then?

Paul: Well, Mum told me all that it was, and I was quite worried about taking the medication. I was told it was a drug like speed or whatever, and . . .

Ian: And what's speed?

Paul: It's a drug.

Ian: And what effect does that have on you?

Paul: I don't know. How am I supposed to know? I've never taken it [laughs].

Ian: So you've never taken speed?

Paul: No way.

Ian: But this drug that you needed to take for ADHD is like speed?

Paul: Yeah. It's Ritalin, and he said it's like speed, but I wasn't too keen on it at first.

Ian: Why were you not keen on it at first?

Paul: I don't know. You kind of hear "speed" and think of the illegal drug, and back then I was twelve, thirteen. . . .

Ian: So you thought you were being asked to take an illegal drug. Did you think you'd be on heroin next?

Paul: [Laughs] Yeah. I kept asking Mum questions about it.

Ian: What questions did you ask her?

Paul: I don't know. That was ages ago.

Ian: Why do you think you wanted to know more about it?

Paul: I don't know—just to see if it was safe, I suppose.

Ian: So you were kind of worried about what kind of effect this would have on you?

Paul: Yes.

Ian: What kind of effect did this drug have on you?

Paul: When I started to take it, it took away my appetite a lot when I was getting used to it. But it worked; it helped calm me down a bit. But then, because I got used to it, it didn't work.

Ian: What else happened?

Paul: Nothing, really. It just helped me concentrate.

Ian: How did you notice that?

Paul: I didn't. My teachers told my mum about it, and my mum told me. I don't know anything about what happens to me. I have to be told because, like, it's a bit hard to know what's happened if you don't even know if it's working or not.

Ian: Yes. That's why I was asking, because I was wondering if you had noticed any difference. You're saying . . .

Paul: No, I never noticed a thing.

Ian: So you were told that you had hyperactivity and you were told that you were ADHD, and what that meant was that you had to start taking Ritalin, and you were not allowed to have much sugar or dessert. And what you're telling me now is that in the last month you have stopped taking Ritalin and you're eating a lot more sugar, and you say that things are no different from before a month ago.

Paul: Yeah.

Ian: So do you think that hyperactivity and ADHD are two descriptions that fit or don't fit you?

Paul: Don't fit me.

Ian: So neither of them fit you?

Paul: No [pp. 294–298].

Ian and Paul's interview is a good illustration of deconstruction at work. Ian explores and unpacks Paul's meanings about ADHD and Ritalin. It is clear that the ADHD label did not capture his interest or experience. The label was an experience that was imposed on him. He formed a view of himself that meant he was unable to take full responsibility for himself due to a biological disorder. By asking Paul some deconstructing questions, Ian quickly established that the ADHD label didn't fit Paul. After shedding the ADHD label, Ian's interview progressed to an exploration of areas of Paul's life outside the ADHD label—areas of competence and personal agency.

Case Example: Unpacking ADHD with Mom

Teri was a thirty-one-year-old single parent of seven-year-old Jesse. Jesse, an energetic and creative boy, was evaluated by his pediatrician for ADHD and placed on Ritalin. The referral was due to teacher reports that Jesse was distractible and hyper. In addition, Teri, recently divorced, was having a challenging time managing his behavior. The doctor referred Teri to a class for parents of ADHD children so that she could receive information on how to raise a hyperactive child. In that class (which she found helpful), she found out about CHADD. After the four sessions of the class ended, she began attending CHADD. Jesse's pediatrician also referred Jesse and Teri to me for family therapy because, even with Ritalin, things had not improved much.

In my conversations with Teri, she said that she found the CHADD group "supportive . . . that she felt she wasn't alone." Jesse's receiving the diagnosis of ADHD was welcome relief for Teri; she no longer felt guilty or incompetent as a parent. Yet she felt that Jesse's behavior had not improved much, even with Ritalin, the class, and CHADD. Jesse was not much interested in therapy at the beginning. He typically responded to my questions with "I don't know." I mostly worked with Teri in the initial stage of treatment.

The ensuing transcript is a deconstructing conversation she and I had. Jesse was not in the room at the time.

David: You have found the CHADD group helpful right?

Teri: Yes, I don't feel so alone. I don't feel that I am a bad parent anymore.

David: So, CHADD has been a welcome relief from mother-blame and guilt?

Teri: Yes, unquestionably! It's been helpful for me. But all this stuff doesn't mean much to Jesse. I wonder if he even knows what ADHD means. And he is still not listening to me. His teacher said that his attention is a little better but not much. Maybe Ritalin isn't the only answer.

David: Perhaps. Is that a new realization?

Teri: Yes. I have been getting a lot out of this ADHD stuff . . . but I don't think it makes a difference to him.

David: Have you ever wondered if Jesse thinks that taking Ritalin means he is stupid or crazy?

Teri: Yes, I do wonder about that. In fact, he has said that some of the kids make fun that he has to take a pill.

David: What do you think it would mean to Jesse if he felt that having the label of ADHD means that he had to settle for less in life? That he didn't have many talents?

Teri: Well, I wouldn't want that. I would be concerned of course. Do you think that might be going on?

David: I don't know. I do know that other kids have told me that.

Teri: Hmm . . .

David: Many of these kids have enormous talents, but teachers and doctors don't discuss them much. Teri, in your CHADD groups, do they ever talk about the unique talents and abilities of ADHD children? Or do they just focus on deficits?

Teri: You know, I have never heard anything positive about the kids. It's all diseases, brain stuff . . .

David: What message do you think Jesse might receive if he heard how they (CHADD groups) talk about kids?

Teri: Well, it could mean he is, as you said, having to settle for less in life.

David: Would you like to give him that message?

Teri: Of course not!

David: Do you have any ideas about how you might reduce the likelihood that Jesse is flawed? And remember, I know his behavior is really, really challenging at times. But I wonder whether, if he has the message that he is flawed, it might inadvertently feed the problem. I am wondering what it might do for Jesse if you gave as much attention to the talents that you said he had when you filled out the SMART scale as to the problems you checked off on the Connors Rating Scale.

Teri: I imagine it would improve his self-esteem.

After this conversation, I redirected the focus of therapy on Jesse's talents, which were many. Jesse became more involved in therapy. Teri continued to attend CHADD groups but took them with a grain of salt. She said she did benefit from some of the CHADD information but discarded the rest. A significant step was when Teri gave a speech at one of the CHADD meetings. Her topic was "Nurturing the Unique Abilities of ADHD children." Evidently, many parents came up to her after her talk and thanked her, saying they agreed with her critique but had been afraid to say so in the CHADD meetings.

———

This chapter illustrates the key practice of mapping the effects of ADHD. By asking both effects questions and deconstructing questions, the problem of ADHD is further separated from the child. Once this occurs, times when the child has taken effective action against the effects of ADHD can be noticed—the focus of our next chapter.

Chapter Six

Step Three

Attending to Exceptions to the ADHD Story

After mapping the influence that ADHD has over the child and family, we shift gears and begin working with the family to map the influence that the child and family have over ADHD. We do this by looking for incidents of past success in dealing with the problem. We explore times when the child has made preferred choices, resisted ADHD behaviors, and surprised parents, teachers, and friends with his excellent attention or self-control.

Similarly, we explore times when parents or siblings have re-sisted the problem-saturated ADHD story. I call these exceptions to the problem story. Exceptions refer to times when the child or family have taken effective action against ADHD (Chang, 1998; de Shazer, 1985; Walter and Peller, 1992). Michael White (1991, p. 16) refers to exceptions as "unique outcomes." Exceptions or unique outcomes provide an entry point into an alternative, pre-ferred story.

For example, in *The Adventures of Huckleberry Finn*, the Widow Douglas was quite concerned that Huck has no interest in school. She developed a problem-saturated story that Huck was not capa-ble of being civilized. Yet in the novel, Huck does go to school and even learns to read and write. He becomes more determined to at-tend school to spite his father. This would qualify as an exception or unique outcome—a contradiction to the problem story. Michael White (1991) states that these unique outcomes (or exceptions) may be actions, intentions to act, moments when the effects of the problem don't seem so strong, or areas of life that remain unaffected by the problem.

An exception may also be a time when the child is on a constant dosage of Ritalin and is able to focus and concentrate in class without a corresponding increase in the medication. Often the problem may occur only at home or at school, or vice versa, or may *not* have been exacerbated during a break from taking Ritalin (Law, 1997). By being curious about these gaps or contradictions to the ADHD story, it becomes possible to elicit a story of personal agency and competency. This chapter focuses on ways to find and elaborate on exceptions to the problem story. Case examples portray this step in the SMART approach.

Questions About Exceptions

As an externalizing conversation develops, SMART therapists are alert to any exception to the problem story. Sometimes children mention an exception or demonstrate it spontaneously in a session. Often the child or family barely notices the exception because it seems trivial compared to the gravity of the symptoms they are experiencing. But as SMART therapists, we learn how problems trick people into forgetting their own competencies. We ask questions about these moments. We try to determine whether the client prefers the problem behavior or the exception behavior. If the client prefers the exception, we ask questions to elicit a competency-based narrative.

After determining collaboratively that an exception is a preference, we then ask the child what kind of relationship he would like to have with ADHD. Sometimes the child selects a power-over-the-problem metaphor such as "fighting ADHD," "defeating ADHD," or "beating up on the Hyper Monster." Other times the child may favor a metaphor of power in relation to the problem (Freeman, Epston, and Lobovits, 1997). These metaphors may include agreement, harmony, or balance with the problem.

Power-in-relation-to-the-problem metaphors may be particularly useful with ADHD. Because ADHD may involve at least some biological factors, a complete "cure" might not be possible. In fact, ADHD may have some desirable effects such as energy and creativity. As a result, metaphors that reflect coming into harmony with ADHD may be more effective in helping the young person establish greater control over ADHD's undesired effects. One useful metaphor is "befriending the positive aspects (such as energy) of ADHD" to use for good purposes.

If we do not notice exceptions, we ask questions to determine whether there has been a time in the past when ADHD had less influence. SMART therapists assume that there are always exceptions to the ADHD story, even if they seem hard to locate. We listen for gaps or contradictions and then politely interrupt and ask about them. If the child is too humble to notice his competency, we ask others in his life to do so (parents, siblings, classmates, teachers, and so on).

Here are a few examples of exception questions that I might ask a child. (I discuss exception questions for parents later in this chapter.)

Has there been a time when ADHD could have taken control in the classroom but didn't?

Are there times when you pay attention, even when the teacher is boring?

What's different about the times you do your homework, even when your parents don't remind you?

Did ADHD want you to come to this session? Why is ADHD worried that you are coming here to see me?

Even though ADHD told you not to go to school today, you went anyway. Is that a positive or negative event? Why or why not?

Does ADHD ever take a break?

Even though ADHD tries to tell you that you're dumb, you believe that you are good at computers. Does this suggest that ADHD does not fully claim your life?

Why hasn't ADHD totally convinced you that you have to settle for less in life? Do you see a future that is yours and not ADHD's?

What kind of relationship would you like with ADHD? Would you like to get the upper hand with it, trick it, stand up to it, or balance yourself in relation to ADHD?

What parts of ADHD are friendly to you, and what parts do you a disservice? What would you like to do with the parts of ADHD that are a disservice to you?

Case Example: Brendan Revisited

You may recall my conversation with Brendan in Chapter Five in which we mapped the influence of ADHD on his life. There was a point in the conversation when Brendan stated that ADHD had not totally convinced him that he is dumb. He said that in spite of ADHD he just does the work. Brendan even said the work wasn't so hard. This statement may qualify as an exception or unique outcome. I ask him and his father, Jack, about this possible exception:

> *David:* A few minutes ago, Brendan, you mentioned that ADHD has not completely convinced you that you are dumb. Is that right?
>
> *Brendan:* Yes.
>
> *David:* You said, "I just do the work." Is that right? [Brendan nods yes.] Can I ask about that? Is this positive—that you can do the work and it's not so hard?
>
> *Brendan:* I guess so.
>
> *David:* So you think it is positive. Why do you think it is positive?
>
> *Brendan:* Because I am not so dumb after all. I can do the work, even social studies.

David: Wow! What does ADHD think of your ability to do the work?

Brendan: It does *not* like it at all!

David: Why?

Brendan: Well, if ADHD had its way, I wouldn't do any work and just be a bum and get kicked out of every school.

David: Does this mean that you want to stay in school, even against ADHD's wishes?

Brendan: Yeah.

David: Why do you want to go to school? Isn't it boring?

Brendan: Yeah, it's boring, but I want a job, dude!

David: What kind of job?

Brendan: A job that makes serious cash! I am good at computers . . . maybe a computer job.

David: Did you know this, Jack?

Jack: Yes. He's awesome at the computer and at math.

David: He is, huh?

Jack: Yes.

David: Brendan, I am hearing things that don't quite fit with ADHD's plot against you. You can do the work, even social studies; you are good at the computer; you think about the future; you are good at math. Wow! How do you do this? How do you do the work?

Brendan: I just sit down in my room and do it.

David: Jack, how does he do it? I mean, ADHD gets kids to *not* focus and do the work. What does it say about Brendan that he can do the work if he wants to? Help me make sense of this!

Jack: Well, he is bright. He reads *National Geographic* all the time. He has stacks and stacks of them in his room. He can be really curious.

David: So, Brendan would it be fair to say that ADHD is not completely winning in its plot against you—that you have a plot against ADHD?

Brendan: Yes.

David: Since you are good at math, what percentage out of 100 percent is ADHD running the show, and what percentage are you in charge?

Brendan: I would say ADHD 55 percent and me 45 percent.

David: Wow! So you have 45 percent. What if you built on that 45 percent? What would it mean for ADHD? Do you think it would be kicked out of school instead of you?

Brendan: Yeah, I think so!

David: ADHD would have you kicked out of every school in the universe. But with you plotting against it, do you think you are pioneering a new direction in your school career?

Brendan: Yes.

David: What do you think, Jack?

Jack: Oh, most definitely!

The rest of the session focused on describing and elaborating on Brendan's talents that have enabled him to have 45 percent success in relationship to ADHD. Drawing on his computer and math talents, I asked him to make a pie chart on the computer depicting his relationship with ADHD (see Figure 6.1).

The remainder of my therapy with Brendan focused on resurrecting his abilities and gaining more influence over ADHD. His

Figure 6.1. Brendan's Plot Against ADHD.

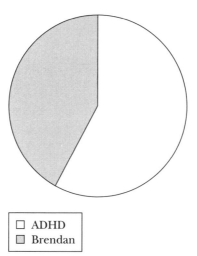

☐ ADHD
☐ Brendan

grades and behavior significantly improved in school. Each time we meet, the percentage of the pie for Brendan increases. We printed out each pie chart as visual documentation of his progress.

The Detective Club

Winslade and Monk (1999) state that an effective therapist "needs to be alert to the discovery of clues to competence. Like a detective trying to build a case from what at first seems like little available evidence, a counselor combs carefully through the problem-saturated story for openings to a different story" (p. 41).

Family therapist Debora Brooks (personal communication, 1998) developed a similar practice in her work with families that she calls The Detective Club. Debora noticed that ADHD seems to rob families of any awareness of their skills, talents, and abilities. She observed how the serious and painful effects of ADHD tricked families into minimizing and discounting their moments of resistance to the powers of ADHD. To counter these effects, Debora formed The Detective Club. All family members are invited to become members of the club, and therapy sessions take the form of club meetings.

During the first meeting of the club, each family member is provided with a small notebook and a pencil. Debora volunteers to take the meeting's "minutes" on a large piece of butcher paper, which is posted for all club members to see. Debora begins the meeting by asking the family questions about the culprit, ADHD, and the caper it has pulled off by tricking the family into thinking ADHD is in charge. Debora carefully notes the family's observations of when ADHD is in charge.

Next, Debora tells the family that in her experiences with other families, she's noticed that ADHD tricks people into thinking it is always in charge. She asks (playfully) if this is true of this family. Is ADHD *always* in charge? Probably not. Debora challenges the family to become detectives during the next week, investigating times when ADHD is not in charge.

At this point Debora tells the family that, because ADHD is very tricky, it may be difficult for them to see through ADHD's hoax and find evidence of the family's resistance. She asks the family what kinds of skills are necessary to be a good detective, such as being able to listen, watch, and think creatively about problems. She asks the family whether anyone in the family has any of these kinds of skills already and whether the family is interested in using any of those skills to defeat ADHD.

As the meeting progresses, Debora turns the discussion to the qualities, skills, and talents of each family member that might be obscured by ADHD's effects. Then she asks each family member to be on the look-out over the next week for those and other exceptions to ADHD's grasp on the family. She suggests that everyone keep track of their observations in their notebook and be ready to report on their findings at the next session. Finally, she asks the family to come up with a signal, such as a handshake or a motto, to close the session with. She suggests that family members use this signal during the week as they notice exceptions to the problem story.

Members of The Detective Club report back in subsequent meetings about times when ADHD lost its power over the family. The club forms a structure in which families build expertise at noticing their strengths and competencies and shifts the focus of therapy from failures and defeats to successes and victories.

I have adopted Debora's idea with some of the families I work with. For example, I was seeing a single-parent mother, Ruth, and her two ADHD sons, John (eight) and Doug (ten). Ruth was frustrated with Doug's and John's bickering, not listening, and fighting over homework; she was tired of their messy rooms. In an externalizing conversation, Ruth said that ADHD made her children zone out. This frustration led Ruth to raise her voice and yell at her children. As a response to the yelling, Doug and John yelled back, leading to a reciprocal pattern, with ADHD in charge.

Ruth and her children were excited about The Detective Club idea. Doug was particularly excited because he wanted to be a police officer. I encouraged the family to be good detectives and pay attention to any small evidence that Doug was policing his own homework rather than his mother being the homework police. Ruth was asked to pay attention to any hints that her kids were cleaning their rooms. Doug and John were asked to notice over the next two weeks what Mom was doing that made ADHD less powerful.

This assignment inspired the family to find their creativity and humor. Doug and John wrote in The Detective Club book that Mom was "yelling less." Ruth reported that her kids initiated their own homework four times in two weeks. Also, to Ruth's astonishment, they cleaned their rooms without being asked. On other occasions her children answered her on first request rather than zoning out. I awarded Ruth, Doug, and John Detective Club badges for their excellent efforts at finding "anti-ADHD evidence." Ruth turned in her homework police badge for the Detective Club badge!

Making the Child the Expert

Traditional therapy with ADHD kids claims that therapeutic change is slow and arduous. In contrast, the following case example illustrates how externalizing the problem and inviting children to become their own experts can bring brief and powerful changes. In SMART therapy conversations, children begin to experience themselves differently. Instead of being viewed as children with a defect, a SMART therapy conversation enables young persons to experience themselves as knowledgeable and competent. By respecting their ideas and knowledge, rapid and dramatic change is possible.

Case Example: Manuel Sends Trouble to Prison

Manuel, age eleven, was seen with his mother, Leticia, and his stepfather, Michael, due to severe behavioral problems at school and home. At school he was flunking every class except physical education. He had earned a reputation as a troublemaker due to fighting, not listening to the teacher, and being truant. According to Leticia, Manuel was lazy, messy, and argumentative at home. He and his stepfather frequently quarreled.

Manuel had a long-standing diagnosis of ADHD, combined type. He had been on and off Ritalin for five years and was taking it at the time I saw him. Manuel and his family had been to therapy several times without success. Due to their previous therapy experiences and the intensity and history of the problem, Leticia had little hope that things could change. They came to me because they had heard from a friend that I did a different kind of therapy. Leticia told me in the first interview, "I thought we'd give it one more shot. What have we got to lose?"

In the first interview Manuel called the problem Trouble. When I asked him some effects questions, he said that Trouble was making his life a mess and ultimately would lead him toward prison. Manuel said Trouble was in charge of his life 98 percent of the time. I experienced Manuel as engaged in the session as I playfully talked about the effects of Trouble on his life. He said he was ready to make some changes and get Trouble away from him.

Between sessions I asked Leticia and Manuel to play close attention to any small evidence of change (similar to The Detective Club approach). They came back with some spectacular news. The following is our conversation in the second session, which took place two weeks after the initial interview:

David: So, the last time we met up, you said Trouble was running your life 98 percent of the time. Manuel only had 2 percent. Now, two weeks later, you say that you have 50 percent of your own territory. This means you have shrunk Trouble 48 percent! What do you make of this Leticia? Do you see this as positive?

Leticia: Yes. He has been really making an effort. I'm shocked!

David: You're shocked. So am I. I have to ask you about this, Manuel. Is that OK?

Manuel: Sure.

David: Is it positive that you have gone from 2 to 50 percent?

Manuel: Positive.

David: Why is it positive?

Manuel: Because I am acting a lot better.

David: How are you acting better?

Manuel: Well, I made a mess in my room and I cleaned it up.

David: You cleaned up your room? With or without being asked?

Manuel: Without being asked.

David: No way! I remember last time you said Trouble was making a mess of your life. Now you are cleaning up your room. Does this mean you are cleaning out your life? Are you cleaning up for a life without Trouble?

Manuel: Yes.

David: Why did you clean your room? I mean Trouble and its best friend ADHD wanted you to keep your room a mess, I imagine.

Manuel: I like my room. It was a mess and I thought I should clean it.

David: Leticia, were you shocked?

Leticia: Yes. I usually find his room un-vacuumable.

David: What did his room look like this time?

Leticia: Almost immaculate. I couldn't believe it!

David: Did you know your mom was shocked in a positive way?

Manuel: Yes.

David: What else have you been doing to get to 50 percent?

Manuel: I haven't been making a mess when I eat.

David: You used to make a mess?

Manuel: Yeah. Michael hated me for making a mess!

David: Is that true Michael?

Michael: Yeah. He'd leave a piece of pizza over on the couch. Another piece in his bed. It would make me so frustrated.

David: And what are you noticing now?

Michael: He eats at the dinner table and puts his dishes away.

David: Is this true?

Manuel: Yes. I eat my ice cream now over my plate!

David: What? Eating over your plate! What does Trouble think of this?

Manuel: [laughs]

David: Michael, what do you think Trouble thought of Manuel eating over his plate?

Michael: I think Trouble is in trouble!

David: Manuel, is Trouble getting troubled by your commitment to cleaning up your life—of trying to live a clean life instead of a prison life?

Manuel: Yes it is [laughing]!

David: How did you defy Trouble?

Manuel: I just did it. I don't know [continues to laugh] . . . it wasn't too hard.

David: What is going on here Michael? What's different?

Michael: He's being more conscious?

David: What does conscious mean, Manuel?

Manuel: It means being more aware.

David: Is being aware a good thing?

Manuel: Yes.

David: Did Trouble's friend, ADHD, make you aware or not aware?

Manuel: Not aware.

David: How have you been making yourself so aware?

Manuel: I'm just using my brainpower now.

David: Before, was ADHD stealing your brainpower?

Manuel: Yes, but now I have it back!

David: You sure seem to. Do you think you are becoming more aware of the effects Trouble and ADHD were having on your life?

Manuel: Yes.

David: Where were you headed with Trouble and ADHD in charge?

Manuel: A druggie, prison life.

David: A career in prison?

Manuel: Yes.

David: Now what kind of career do you see for yourself?

Manuel: A good one.

David: Any other exceptions to Trouble?

Manuel: Are there any other steps I am taking, Mom?

Leticia: He hasn't been as argumentative.

David: What's different? Can you give me an example?

Leticia: Well, I tested him the other day by sitting on the couch and asking him to do things for me. He didn't argue back.

David: Manuel, is this true—that you didn't get angry or argumentative when your mother engaged in Trouble testing.

Manuel: Yes!

David: Is this positive?

Manuel: Yes.

David: Why?

Manuel: I'm growing up.

David: You're growing up, eh?

Leticia: He also seems happier overall.

David: How do you make sense of this, Leticia?

Leticia: I think he has really been thinking since the first time you met with us. I see light at the end of the tunnel.

David: You have hope?

Manuel: Yes.

David: Now that you have hope, what do you want to do to Trouble?

Manuel: I want to put it in prison!

David: Do you think you have enough grounds to put Trouble away?

Manuel: Yes.

David: If the old story was Trouble in charge, what's the new story?

Manuel: Manuel has 50 percent of his territory back from Trouble.

David: That is awesome!

The dialogue between Manuel and me then centered on ways he could apply his Trouble-taming abilities at school. Both his home and school life significantly improved. At our last session (of six sessions in all), he was in charge 90 percent, with Trouble having a "measly 10 percent."

Parents as Exception Finders

As stated previously, some parents are invested in the ADHD diagnosis because it absolves them of guilt. Once recruited into the dominant medical discourse about ADHD, parents turn the problem over to an expert authority to manage. Parents typically think that neither they nor their child can manage the problem on their own; their sense of personal agency may not be available to them after years of receiving judgment and advice from teachers and professionals.

Because the ADHD story can be powerful and totalizing, a child's competencies or exceptions (which often appear in disguised form) can be overlooked. But unless parents can recognize exceptions and applaud them, it is practically impossible to construct an alternative story that is as potent as the ADHD story. The new story of competency can only take hold if there is an audience, such as parents and teachers, to appreciate it. It is critical in this approach to encourage parents to become aware of and appreciate the exceptions to the ADHD.

Case Example: Derek's Mom Finds Exceptions

This was the case with Janine, a single-parent mother of Derek, age eleven, who was diagnosed with ADHD, hyperactive-impulsive type. Derek was having problems at school with his temper and found it hard to follow instructions and pay attention in class. He was barely passing the sixth grade when they came to see me. Janine was very concerned about Derek and worried that he would end up like his father—an alcoholic who had a hard time holding down a job. Derek's father was drinking heavily at the time of their therapy with me.

I found Derek to be a very creative, albeit active young person. He was talented at sports and artwork; he had many friends. He stated that he found school to be "a drag . . . very boring." Typically, he and his mother would argue over his homework and chores. Janine stated that she was very frustrated over always having to remind Derek of his responsibilities. Derek was equally frustrated with his mother's nagging. When I asked Janine about exceptions to the problem, she was unable to locate one. The ADHD story was so totalizing that it was a challenge to think of a time when Derek was in control of ADHD. Jeanine rather dejectedly told me, "Because of Derek's ADHD, I don't think he will be able to go to college."

When parents are unable to notice exceptions or they minimize the ones they do notice, I often give them a handout written by solution-focused Linda Metcalf (1997) titled, "Looking for Exceptions with Energetic Kids." The handout encourages parents to be vigilant for any small sign of an exception.

Here are the questions on the handout:

Home Life

If you followed your child around each day this week, twenty-four hours a day, in what places, situations, or with whom would you find him paying attention and behaving slightly better? What seems to work in these situations, slightly? Ask your child for this information.

If you were to watch your child today very closely and notice the times when he stays on task for a few minutes longer, would he require your constant reminders, or would he need a note taped to the bedroom door to remind him of one thing to do? Watch! What seems to work with your child, according to him?

In your family, which parent is successful at encouraging your child to complete a task more efficiently? What does that person do that seems to work? Ask your child what seems to make the difference.

Social Life

As you look back over the years, were there times when he paid attention better and had few-to-no behavior problems? What was happening then at home, with friends, or at school that made things easier? What would your child say?

In which situations does your child get along socially? Does he play better one-on-one or in a group of many or few children? Write these down and ask your child which is easier for him.

School Life

Recall times during your child's school career when he did well in school behaviorally and academically. What was different during that time? What were his teachers like—his friends, his routine? What did you do that helped? List the school year, the teachers, and, together with your child, talk about what you both think seemed to make a difference so that school was successful.

Which school subjects does your child do well at? List them below. Beside each subject, ask your child what the teacher does that keeps his interest. Where does he sit in the classroom that seems to work? Ask your child what the teacher (and the subject) does for him personally that makes school fun and interesting. The answers will tell you how he learns best [pp. 131–132].

Three weeks later Jeanine returned with the handout filled out. She said the questions were "very helpful . . . they helped me remember Derek in a more positive light." As I asked about this, Jeanine shared with me that she recalled Derek doing better in school in the fourth grade. She attributed his past academic success to his fourth grade school teacher, Mr. Davis. Apparently, Mr. Davis took a special interest in Derek and helped him pursue his interest in painting and artwork. In addition, Mr. Davis's teaching style was very active and kept Derek's attention. For instance, he would have people dress up in costume to play different characters from the book they were reading. Derek discovered that he had a talent in acting. Derek also sat in the front of the classroom that year. In sixth grade he was sitting way in the back.

I asked Derek and Jeanine where ADHD was that year. They both stated, "It took a vacation!" Jeanine also stopped reminding Derek of his homework and posted a note to his bedroom door, as was suggested in the handout. Apparently, this idea worked fabulously, to Jeanine's surprise. Derek initiated his homework every day after she put the note up. Derek appreciated that his mother was no longer nagging him.

Last, the handout reminded Jeanine that Derek was doing better behaviorally about a year ago. At that time Derek's father was not drinking and was consistently seeing Derek. She made the connection that Derek's behavior problems are possibly related to his relationship with his father. This allowed her to stop viewing ADHD as a completely biological problem.

The handout helped Jeanine see exceptions to Derek's problems. She became more tolerant of his behavior and highlighted his strengths. Jeanine also became an advocate for Derek. For instance, she talked to Derek's sixth grade teacher and shared her thoughts on what teaching strategies engage her son. The teacher heard Jeanine's critique and readjusted his teaching strategies; he even put Derek in the front of the classroom. Derek's grades improved and the ADHD diagnosis was rendered irrelevant.

Overcoming a Reputation

Because ADHD tends to show up often in classrooms, it is important to have teachers notice exceptions to the ADHD story. Quite often the student diagnosed with ADHD has developed a reputation as a troublemaker or poor student. This reputation can be overpowering and can make it difficult for teachers to notice small but significant changes.

Case Example: Scott Alerts His Teachers

Such was the case with Scott, a thirteen-year-old diagnosed with ADHD, combined type. He had earned a reputation as a trouble-maker due to his "attitude." He disrupted the class with inappropriate humor, did not pay attention, did not do his homework, and got into fights at recess. As I engaged Scott in an externalizing conversation about the troublemaker reputation he had earned, he came to the sudden insight that "Troublemaker was dogging him" and did not have his best interests at heart.

As our therapy progressed, Scott had a desire to escape Trouble-maker and rework his reputation. He told me he was making efforts to stay out of Trouble's way (by turning in his homework and not disrupting the class, for example) but was frustrated that his teachers were not noticing. It became clear that his reputation was so thick and long-standing that his teachers were not seeing the recent exceptions. We then decided to co-draft a letter to his teachers announcing his intentions to escape Trouble and build a new reputation (see Chapter Eight for more on letters and therapeutic counter-documentation). The letter served the purpose of alerting his teachers to be vigilant for signs of change.

Here is the letter we sent out to his teachers:

Dear awesome teachers of Scott:

Scott is working with me in counseling to go free of Trouble and its friend ADHD. Scott has come to the realization that he has built a troublemaking reputation due to

- Not doing his work

- Grades below "C" level

- Disrupting the class

- An attitude problem

- Fighting

Scott has decided that Trouble is "dogging him" and keeping him from a future of his own designs. He clearly told me he wants to change and is beginning to make small steps.

Since the troublemaker reputation has followed Scott around since he was seven, it may be challenging for him to give it the slip. It also might be hard for others to notice any small but significant steps that Scott is taking.

Scott told me that he is going to change his reputation at school. He wants a *responsible reputation*. Scott is asking if you would be so kind as to join his team. Could you please notice any efforts Scott is making to change his reputation? These efforts may include

- Handing in his homework on time

- Improving his grades

- Listening in class

- Staying out of fights

Many thanks for helping Scott and me!
        Sincerely,
        David Nylund, LCSW

After the letter was sent out to his teachers, Scott continued to rework his reputation. He and his mother told me that his teachers were noticing the exceptions to Trouble and ADHD. This noticing helped assemble a new story for Scott that stood up to the old one.

This chapter demonstrates the key step of *attending to exceptions* to the ADHD story. These exceptions became the fuel for a robust alternative story—a story of ability and personal agency. Let's move ahead to step 4. The plot thickens!

Chapter Seven

Step Four

Reclaiming Special Abilities of Children Diagnosed with ADHD

In *The Adventures of Huckleberry Finn*, the Widow Douglas depicts Huck as uncivilized and not interested in school. Early in the novel, he meets up with his alcoholic father, Pap. Pap orders his son not to attend school or visit the Widow Douglas. In spite of Pap's demands, Huck attends school regularly and learns to read and write. Furthermore, he visits the Widow Douglas's place often, which angers Pap. He kidnaps Huck and takes him to his own private cabin where he controls and frequently beats him. Huck decides to protest his father's abuse by running away. He slaughters a pig and uses its blood to fake his own death; he eventually finds a canoe and heads down the Mississippi River.

These events constitute an exception to the story that Huck is uncivilized and not interested in school. He evens attends school knowing Pap will beat him. A SMART therapist working with Huck would be interested in this exception. By asking questions about the meaning of it, we would build a new story for Huck (this technique will be further demonstrated in Chapter Eleven)—a story that tells of his ingenuity, creativity, courage, and preferences. The development of this new story would weaken the influence of the problem story.

The greatest task for the SMART therapist is taking an exception—a sparkling moment when the client triumphed over ADHD—and building a vigorous alternative story that stands up to the power of the ADHD story. The ADHD story typically grows over time and takes on a life of its own. The family, supported by discourses in psychiatry, psychotherapy, and the media, can believe that the ADHD story speaks to the truth of their child's identity. In this environment one or two isolated experiences are not going to accomplish the goal of rebuilding an alternative story. Neither will positive talk or cheerleading stop the invasion of the problem.

The skill in using the SMART approach lies in "carefully assembling, with the client, a story line that is invigorating, colorful and compelling" (Winslade and Monk, 1999, p. 44). This alternative story emerges through mapping the effects of ADHD and eliciting exceptions. As stated in Chapter Six, these exceptions can appear in subtle and concealed forms and are often overlooked or minimized by families. If we wait for the child or parent to volunteer the competency-based story, we may never hear it.

The SMART therapist needs to seize on any sparkling moment and respectfully and actively ask "restorying questions" (Zimmerman and Dickerson, 1996, p. 304). Restorying questions help children *reclaim their special abilities* from ADHD. These questions thicken the new story (or counterplot) by giving the child a sense of personal agency. Through this line of inquiry, the child's unique talents, hopes, preferences, intentions, and values are unearthed. Once these talents and strengths are retrieved, the ADHD story loses its hold over the child and family, who literally reclaim their preferred identities. In the following section I discuss ways to develop a counterstory.

Restorying Questions

Restorying questions are divided into three overlapping categories: (1) landscape-of-action questions, (2) landscape-of-meaning questions, and (3) re-membering questions. Let's look at each type in detail.

Landscape-of-Action Questions

Michael White (White and Epston, 1990; Freedman and Combs, 1996), following the work of Jerome Bruner (1986), speaks of the dual landscapes of *action* and *meaning*. He says that life-shaping stories evolve in both of these landscapes and therapists should explore both (Freedman and Combs, 1996). The term *landscape of action* (Bruner, 1986) refers to a sequence of events in a story that unfold over time, according to particular plots. Landscape-of-action questions are asked when an exception is pinpointed. Rather than letting the client rest with a general response such as "I don't know" or "I just did it," these questions encourage the child and family to situate exceptions to the problem story in a series of specific events and actions. They imply personal agency by asking the child *how* he achieved these actions. We gently persist with these questions, even when the child doesn't see himself as responsible for the event or gives someone or something else the credit (such as to Ritalin). Asking the child to give an explicit account of how he contributed to the sparkling moment helps the child experience himself as an "actor in his own life" (Winslade and Monk, 1999, p. 44). The child has an opportunity to tell a new story about himself—a success story rather than an ADHD story.

Here are some examples of landscape-of-action questions:

Questions for the Child

When Boredom tried to take advantage of you in the classroom, how did you use it as opportunity to pay attention?

How did you get yourself ready to take this step of paying attention in class?

What special preparations went into getting yourself ready to attack Boredom before it attacked you?

Is there a history of you paying attention when you need to?

As you have more victories over Boredom, how will your life look in five years? What role will ADHD have in your life at that time?

So you took your energy and redirected it onto the ballfield. How have you been channeling your ADHD for your aims now?

How did you initiate your homework without being asked?

Questions for the Parents

How do you think Jimmy went a whole week without a discipline note from his teacher?

How do you explain that Jimmy is listening to his teacher (and to you) in spite of being off Ritalin?

What are you doing as parents to assist Jimmy in strengthening his concentration?

How did you stay so cool when Jimmy's Temper Tantrum was so high?

Does staying cool strengthen or weaken the life of his Temper Tantrum?

Landscape-of-Meaning Questions

Bruner (1986) refers to the *landscape of meaning* as "that imaginary territory where people plot the meanings, desires, intentions, beliefs, commitments, motivations, values, and the like that relate to their experiences in the landscape of action" (Freedman and Combs, 1996, p. 96). Landscape-of-meaning questions encourage children and families to reflect on and give meaning to the positive developments that have occurred in the landscape of action. By asking the client to address, specifically, the meaning they are making about themselves or new events, we underscore the meaning of the new story and further expand the client's experience of their preferred identity.

Here are some illustrations:

Questions for the Child

Let's reflect a bit on these recent positive steps. What does it tell you about yourself that you are staying out of Trouble's way?

Jimmy, what does it say about your goals for your future that you are paying attention in class?

What does it mean that you are listening to your mother and not talking back to her?

In being able to harness your energy into something positive, are you discovering something about yourself that is important to know?

Who would not be surprised that you took this step?

What does your teacher know about you that enabled her to predict that you could take this step?

Questions for the Parents

What hidden abilities do you think Jimmy has to help him improve his grades to B's when ADHD wanted him to have an F average?

What qualities do you have as parents that enable you to hang in there with Jimmy and be on this team fighting against ADHD?

What positive messages do you think you are sending Jimmy when you tell him that he is capable of doing his homework on his own?

Given how hard it is to refrain from being the homework police, what does it say about you that you are turning responsibility over to Jimmy?

Do you fully appreciate the significance of the steps you and Jimmy are taking?

If you had had a parent such as yourself when you were a kid, what might that have done for ADHD in your life?

What does it say about your intentions and desires for Jimmy's life that you are spending so much time reinforcing the changes that he is making?

Re-Membering Questions

Stephen Madigan (1997) writes that postmodern therapy is about "bringing forth re-remembered alternative selves that are experienced outside the realm of a specified problem identity [such as "Jimmy is an ADHD child"]. The so-called problem identity is not considered a fixed state, nor is it located within the person" (p. 342). He states that problem identities ("being ADHD" is an example) are manufactured over time and are supported by the culture. Madigan says these problem identities are unjust, as they misrepresent the person and describe the person in rather thin ways.

For children who have been misrepresented and wrongly pathologized with the ADHD label, we seek to reclaim a child's preferred identity by asking questions that help the person notice aspects of himself that fall outside the problem's version. This process is referred to as re-membering. By entering into a re-membering conversation, children begin to resurrect their abilities, talents, and competencies. The SMART conversation leads to the person developing an improved version of who they might be (White, 1995).

Re-membering conversations are critical in assembling an alternative story that stands up to the dominant ADHD story because the ADHD story is so dense and so popular in the culture and because it focuses on deficits. Many so-called ADHD kids have extensive psychiatric and educational reports that highlight their deficiencies. Such a focus on deficits reinforces the notion that a child is weird, stupid, a day dreamer, or lazy. Often such children are teased about these qualities and otherwise ridiculed.

Through asking re-membering questions, we invite children to reconsider the idea that they are incompetent. We suggest to ADHD kids that they are much more intelligent than they believe but according to different standards than those recognized in our culture (Nylund and Corsiglia, 1996). It has been my experience that many of these children have creative, special abilities (for example, capacities for imagination, music, sports, dance, spatial awareness, art, and computers) that fall outside the very narrow band our society most values (logic, sitting still, math, and repetitive tasks, for example).

Here's a case in point: Huck Finn was viewed in his time as uncivilized, rebellious, dumb, deceptive, and mischievous. In a remembering conversation, Huck would be invited to appreciate these qualities, as they make him an interesting and a uniquely abled person. These so-called deficit descriptions would be reevaluated and seen as intelligence, creativity, imagination, and courage.

As a way of reinforcing the idea that Huck-like or ADHD kids are gifted, we read positive quotes about ADHD to the families we see. Here are three examples (Gallagher, 1999, p. 1):

> I don't like the term "attention deficit disorder." Although ADHD can generate a host of problems, there are also advantages to having it . . . such as high energy, intuitiveness, creativity, and enthusiasm, and they are completely overlooked by the "disorder" model. The disorder didn't keep me from becoming a doctor, and it hasn't kept many others from far greater success in a wide variety of fields. (Edward Hallowell, M.D.)

> More and more, the concept of ADHD as a disorder is being qualified by inclusion of a string of positive qualities—such as creativity, high intelligence, ability to do many things at once, an aptitude for small business entrepreneurship, and a powerful intuitive sense. (Susan Burgess)

> In my opinion, the ADHD brain structure is not truly an abnormality. In fact, I believe a very good case can be made that it is not only normal but may well be a superior brain structure. However, the talents of the person with ADHD brain structure are not rewarded by our society at its current stage of development. In other words, the problems of the person with ADHD are caused by the way we have our society, educational system, and business methods organized as by other factors more directly related to the ADHD itself. (Paul Elliott, M.D.)

Reading these quotes can be an empowering experience for children and families. After reading them, children often re-member some of their own special talents. To support this re-membering process, I inform them of famous poets, inventors, artists, and creators in history who would be seen as ADHD today (Edison, Mozart, and Einstein, for example).

By asking these questions and reading the quotes, children and parents often come to a very different perspective on their ADHD. Instead of viewing ADHD as a brain defect, families view ADHD as an expression of boredom and frustration with an incompatible environment and unrealistic expectations. ADHD symptoms such as inattention and daydreaming are perceived as tradeoffs for hidden creative abilities such as artistic talent or inventiveness. I often share with families this excerpt from Teresa Gallagher (1999): "Every gift has a trade-off. Stop focusing on the trade-off and learn to recognize your gifts" (p. 1).

When we trace these special abilities back to the source, we often discover what David Epston refers to as "weird abilities" (Freeman, Epston, and Lobovits, 1997, p. 182). These weird abilities reside in the child's inner world, imagination, wizardry, or intuition; they may include imaginary friends, magic, "reading hearts; turning oneself into an imaginary animal; using telepathy to know things in dreams; calming oneself by using juggling skills" (Freeman, Epston, and Lobovits, 1997, p. 183).

When we allow space for children to talk about these weird abilities, their inner experiences become honored in family therapy. Typically, parents' and teachers' ideas have the monopoly on what constitutes ability and knowledge. The SMART approach counters this tendency by privileging the young person's knowledge and ideas about what constitutes ability.

Parents become amazed and proud of their child's unique and hidden talents and begin nurturing, supporting, and celebrating them. Often the parents are inspired to rediscover their own weird abilities that were suppressed when they became adolescents. By commemorating these abilities, the teasing from the other children loses its potency. Often these gifts are then harnessed into good use in overcoming the effects of ADHD. Children become the experts at the solutions.

With re-membering questions, the weight of the ADHD-pathology story dissolves as children and their parents reclaim their lost abilities. As the new story (counterplot) develops, we invite children to give it a name like "Johnny in charge, not ADHD." We then invite family members to watch for more sparkling moments that fit with the counterplot. The rest of the therapy then focuses on cycling through the same process of exception questions and restorying questions. Eventually, the vitality of the counterplot is substantial. It is important to create an audience for the new developments in the child's life (see Chapter Eight). For now, let's look at some examples of re-membering questions:

Questions for the Child

Jimmy, by any chance are you weirdly abled? (Epston, 1997).

What special talents do you think you possess that go unnoticed by your teacher and ADHD?

How does juggling help you to calm your Temper?

How do your imaginary friends help you with homework?

What gifts do you possess that make ADHD want to run for cover?

Now that you have access to your special abilities, what chance does ADHD have to spoil your education?

Your teacher describes you as a daydreamer and says you are out of it. What are you into? Where is your mind at those moments? Is it focusing on something interesting?

Questions for the Parent

Did you know your child possessed these unique gifts?

How have you nurtured these gifts?

If you continue to support and nurture your child's weird abilities, what might happen to ADHD?

Do you remember what weird abilities you had as a child? Did you ever use them to make things better? (Epston, 1997).

If you resurrected your special and weird abilities along with your son, what might these mean for the future of ADHD in your family?

Let's now turn to case examples to illustrate step 4.

Case Example: Sal's Karate Training

Sal was a very intelligent and gifted eleven-year-old who lived with his single-parent father, Mark, and six-year-old sister. He was diagnosed with ADHD, combined type. His presenting problems included temper outbursts at home and included fighting with his sister, being inattentive at school, not completing his homework assignments, having problems sitting still in his seat at school, and goofing off in class.

Mark was very supportive of Sal and attended every session. Sal's ADHD reputation at school concerned him. Mark knew all too well about this. He too was diagnosed with ADHD as a child and barely passed high school. He then took up martial arts and Zen Buddhism, which helped him improve his concentration. He became so successful at it that he earned a fourth-degree black belt in karate. Mark found that the philosophy and values inherent in martial arts and Buddhism—mental discipline, centering one's focus, mindfulness, and self-control—were immeasurable in improving his ability to concentrate. From his martial arts experience, Mark improved his confidence and discovered his hidden talent for working with computers. Mark was a successful computer technician when I saw him and Sal.

In therapy, Sal was inspired to take up karate after hearing his father's story. Mark encouraged it and saw it as an alternative to medication. Sal became quite skilled at karate, which helped his confidence. His grades improved, his temper decreased, and he was able to focus in class, even without Ritalin.

In the following transcript, I inquire about his skills and talents at karate and how they may have contributed to his success at getting the upper hand on ADHD. Mark is in the room with us at the time:

David: So, I understand you have been strengthening your concentration. Has your karate helped you with that?

Sal: I think so.

David: How so?

Sal: Well, my sansei (karate instructor) has been teaching me to focus and improve my mind.

David: Do you take that focus into the classroom?

Sal: Yes.

David: Is it sort of like mental karate?

Sal: Yeah [laughing].

David: I imagine your dad's knowledge of karate has also helped you? [Sal nods yes.] How has he helped?

Sal: He teaches me about karate and what his master taught him. And he reads me cool quotes from books of his. Dad, why don't you read one of those quotes.

Mark: [Dad takes out a book, *Zen in the Martial Arts* by Joe Hyans (1979), and looks up a quote from a Zen Master.] Here is one: "For the uncontrolled there is no wisdom, nor for the uncontrolled is there the power of concentration; and for him without concentration there is no peace."

David: Why did you pick that quote?

Mark: Because karate and Zen help you to concentrate . . . to be mindful. I think that is what is teaching Sal to improve his concentration.

David: Do you think that are any sanseis or Zen masters who have ADHD?

Mark: [Laughing] No way. They have incredible abilities at focusing and centering . . . at slowing down. I know it's helped me enormously.

David: Would you say that you are passing your talent down to your son?

Mark: Yes, I guess I am.

David: Do you fully appreciate this talent the two of you have? It seems to be much better than Ritalin [both laugh]! What does this mean for ADHD?

Mark: I don't think it is as powerful now.

David: Sal, is ADHD a friend or enemy to you now?

Sal: Well, I thought it was an enemy but I think it's a friend now. Dad, you helped me to see it that way. What's that Bruce Lee quote you told me?

Mark: Well yeah, Dave. Michael (Sal's sansei) and I have been teaching him to befriend his ADHD. Yes, it can cause problems such as being hyper and restless and angry, but it's what makes Sal so talented and interesting. He needs to come into harmony with it. Here's the Bruce Lee quote (from the same book): "You and your opponent are one. There is a coexisting relationship between you. You coexist with your opponent and became his complement, absorbing his attack and using his force to overcome him" (Hyans, 1979, p. 51).

David: So, ADHD is the enemy that Sal is coming into harmony or coexistence with?

Mark: Yes.

David: Sal, are you channeling ADHD's energy for your own purposes now?

Sal: Yes, I bring it with me to karate class. I get my energy out there and I feel calmer.

David: Is your mental karate ability helping you to calm your Temper?

Sal: I think so. My sensei says, "Control your anger before it controls you."

David: Did you know you had these special talents?

Sal: No.

David: How do you calm yourself down?

Sal: I just tell my mind to focus, and I think of my sansei.

David: And that helps?

Sal: Yes.

David: Now that you can find access to your calming ability, what does this say about you?

Sal: That I can do anything I want.

David: Would "Doing Anything You Want" be the new story for you?

Sal: Yeah, I guess.

David: And does that new story fit you better than the ADHD story?

Sal: I think so.

David: Is there anything else you are doing to befriend your ADHD and your Temper so it doesn't control you?

Sal: Yeah. My dad lets me have a one-day-a-week blow-out period.

David: What's that?

Sal: I go into my room and for a half-hour I can scream, jump around, get hyper, eat all the sugar and ice cream I want!

David: Wow! Did you come up with that idea?

Sal: Yes.

David: How does it help?

Sal: It gets my Hyperness out.

David: I see! Mark, what does it say about Sal that he came up with this blow-out idea?

Mark: It says that he has a good imagination!

Sal continued to make progress in his karate and in his life. He was able to improve without the aid of medication. His grades significantly improved, as did his reputation at school.

Case Example: Sarah's Imaginary Friend

I saw Sarah, age twelve, and her single-parent mother, Isabel, in a consulting session at a agency where I supervise therapists. Present in the session were several colleagues of mine, Sarah's therapist, and Isabel. Sarah had experienced numerous traumas in her life, including sexual abuse as a child. She had been given many psychiatric diagnoses, including ADHD. Sarah was described as a day dreamer and odd. I found her to be really interesting and creative; she had a talent for poetry and painting.

In spite of these gifts, few people in the school knew about her talents. Sadly, Sarah told me that her teacher from last year called her stupid. She was teased by many of her peers because of her weirdness, even because of her choice in clothes. When I asked her about other weird abilities that caused others to judge her, she told me she had an imaginary friend. This is segment of our conversation:

David: So would it be safe to say that you are weirdly abled?

Sarah: Yes.

David: Do you think others misunderstand you?

Sarah: Yeah, like Ms. Baker (previous teacher). She called me dumb.

David: Do you think you are dumb?

Sarah: No.

David: Are there any other special or weird abilities you have that others misunderstand?

Sarah: Yeah. I talk to a ghost.

David: Is it a friendly ghost or mean ghost?

Sarah: It is a friendly ghost.

David: So it's like an imaginary friend?

Sarah: Yeah. Her name is Trish.

David: And Trish is helpful to you?

Sarah: Yes.

David: How so?

Sarah: She tells me to not argue with my mom. She tells me to do my schoolwork.

David: She does? Is she like an adviser to you—like a constant companion?

Sarah: Yes.

David: How does she help you with your schoolwork?

Sarah: She helps me with math. I hate math! And she helps me to concentrate.

David: She helps you with ADHD?

Sarah: Yes.

David: Does she have any advice about how you should act in class this year?

Sarah: She tells me that I should get B's and pay better attention and not daydream.

David: When you were daydreaming in Ms. Baker's class, what were you thinking of?

Sarah: Oh, I was thinking of Trish or thinking of my poetry or artwork.

David: Was it more interesting than Ms. Baker's lecture?

Sarah: Yes!

David: What does Trish think about Ms. Baker's idea that you are dumb?

Sarah: She doesn't agree. She thinks I am smart and strong.

David: She's helped you with Trauma, too?

Sarah: Yes.

David: And your ADHD?

Sarah: Yes.

David: Isabel, do you know she had these weird abilities?

Isabel: Yes! I had an imaginary friend when I was young, too!

David: You did? I imagine you were told that it was too weird when you got to be Sarah's age?

Isabel: Yes, it wasn't cool.

David: What do you think of Sarah that she has such a close relationship with Trish?

Isabel: I think it's fantastic.

David: What does it say about Sarah that she has the ability to have an imaginary friend?

Isabel: I think it says that she is really creative. And if she has a good teacher, she will do well.

David: If she continues to use Trish as an adviser and believe that she is smart and strong, what might happen to ADHD?

Isabel: I think it would go away.

David: Do you agree, Sarah? Do you think it would fly away like a bad ghost?

Sarah: Yes! It is already gone!

At the end of the consultation session, my colleagues conducted a reflecting team session while Sarah listened in. The team talked about how uniquely abled Sarah was and wished that they had had the gift of an imaginary adviser when they were twelve! These comments appeared to empower Sarah and build up her alternative story. I encouraged her therapist to build on her weird abilities. In addition, I advocated for Sarah's therapist to talk to her about how being a friend to Trish is good training for having real friends.

Case Example: Tracy Takes the Squirmies to Court

Tracy, nine years old, was one of the most spirited, talented, and active children I have ever worked with. He buzzed around my room, picking up things on my desk, playing with my computer, talking constantly, and looking out my window. Often, we met outside so that he could express his boundless energy. I got quite a workout from our sessions!

The reports from school were similar to my experience of Tracy. He said his teacher was always nagging him to slow down, not rush. Tracy also said in the first session: "I am always in trouble for talking!" He had difficulty sitting at his desk and finishing his assignments. Tracy had also developed a strong habit of daydreaming. He creatively named the problem The Squirmies.

His parents, Ellen and Gene, found Tracy's behavior entertaining but, at times, challenging. Ellen told me, "Tracy's a joy to be around . . . most of the time. . . . I just get frustrated when he doesn't clean his room or finish his homework." He often did not hear his parents when they called him; his mind was elsewhere.

The early phase of our therapy focused on Tracy learning to slow down. I spoke to him in a calm, slow voice and taught him to breathe deeply. I accomplished this by having Tracy sit in a chair and close his eyes. Next I asked him to just slow down and notice his breathing and think of something peaceful. Tracy developed his own calming technique: "I think of something calm like the beach and breathe slowly. Then I tell myself, calm down." This exercise appeared to help Tracy slow down and pay attention.

Tracy wanted to be a lawyer when he grew up. We discussed how the Squirmies might keep him from his law degree unless he learned to get authority over it. We collaboratively came up with the idea that he would like to "take the Squirmies to court and put them on trial." I asked if he would like to be an attorney representing himself against the Squirmies. His job was to provide evidence that would prove he was in charge of the Squirmies. I would act as the counsel representing the Squirmies and attempt to provide evidence that they were still in charge.

We set up an appointment for three weeks later. Over the course of the three weeks, he was to build a sound case. I asked him to provide answers to the following questions:

What was your prior relationship with the Squirmies?

What did the Squirmies get you to do?

What kind of reputation did you have?

Can you provide examples when you showed your ability to get
the upper hand on the Squirmies?

During those times, what talents or abilities did you reveal?

Tracy was to include responses to these questions in a closing
argument in front of a jury of his "peers": Tracy's parents, his teacher,
Mr. Davis, and two of my colleagues.

During the course of the next three weeks Tracy tried to learn
everything he could about being a lawyer. He read books, watched
Court TV, and practiced his closing argument. Here is an excerpt
from our next session:

> *Tracy:* Ladies and gentlemen of the jury, I will agree that
> the Squirmies were in charge of me for most of my life. They
> took over my mind and got me to not turn in my work. I
> couldn't sit still, as my legs and arms would go wild. I would
> get mad at kids who would pick on me. At home I wouldn't
> listen to my parents. I was more interested in my Game Boy
> and ignored them when they asked me to take out the trash,
> do my homework, or brush my teeth. My room was a mess. I
> realize that my teacher and other kids thought of me as weird
> or a troublemaker. But I am here to show you that I am in
> charge, *not* the Squirmies. I would like to show the jury this
> picture I took yesterday of my room [shows a Polaroid® shot
> of his room]. Do you see how clean it is? I have been listening
> to my parents and have done my homework. I have brushed
> my teeth and gone to bed on time. I have not gotten mad
> at school, and I am using my calming down technique to
> sit still and listen to my teacher. Ladies and gentlemen of the
> jury, the evidence is clear. I am in charge of the Squirmies!
> I have shown many talents, including being able to
> concentrate. I am stronger and can be in control. I am

smarter than the Squirmies. And I can grow up rather than grow down.

I then made my closing statement as counsel for the Squirmies:

David: Ladies and gentlemen of the jury, Tracy would have you believe that my client, the Squirmies, has lost control of him. I beg to differ. Yes, Tracy has a few minor victories the last three weeks. But my client has been in charge of Tracy for nine years. I urge you not to trust in these recent changes. My client will come back with a vengeance. Tracy has made these temporary changes before. But the Squirmies always come back. Don't be swayed by the photo or his seductive argument. We rest our case.

The jury then went into a private room to deliberate. Tracy and I had taken up our roles quite seriously, and we anxiously awaited their decision. After ten minutes, the jury returned with their verdict. The jury foreman, Ellen, read the decision:

Ellen: The jury found Tracy's argument to be very convincing and eloquent! His evidence was more compelling than the counsel for the Squirmies, particularly the photograph. Tracy's recent behavior, both at home and school, proves that he has many capabilities, weird abilities, and talents. We think the preponderance of evidence is in favor of Tracy. We award Tracy as he has the upper hand 77 percent of the time. The Squirmies only have 23 percent.

Tracy jumped for joy as the decision was read. I—the dejected attorney—congratulated Tracy and then put my therapist hat on. The rest of the therapy focused on building on his special and weird abilities, and exploring the landscape of action and meaning that supported his recent victories over ADHD.

The Child Gets Credit, Not Ritalin

As I stated in Chapter Three, medication often is a central issue in treating kids who have been labeled ADHD. Often, when positive changes occur, all of the credit is given to Ritalin. The child's own personal agency is undermined. This becomes problematic, as the child's abilities and strengths are never discovered or appreciated. As a result, the ADHD biological story stays in charge. The child gets the message that she has no agency or ability without the aid of Ritalin. She is a passive subject to a psychostimulant. To counter this effort, I encourage children and families to locate their own agency alongside the medication.

Case Example: Shawn Gets Credit

Shawn, age twelve (diagnosed with ADHD, inattentive type), was able to improve his attention and his grades with the aid of Ritalin. I interviewed him and his mother, Marlene, at the end of therapy to honor and celebrate the changes he had made. Here is our discussion about his role in the achievements and Ritalin's role:

David: What has been helpful?

Marlene: Of course, the medication he has been on, but that's been the same—a constant throughout.

David: So is it safe to say the medication is not the sole reason for the changes?

Marlene: Oh yeah. If I were to look at it on a scale, the medication was just one point we had to do. There were a lot of things we had to do. Does that make sense? I would say 25 percent medication and 75 percent effort.

Shawn: Actually, probably only 5 percent medication.

David: Wow, only 5 percent?

Shawn: Yeah, 95 percent effort!

Marlene: [Laughs] That's interesting. I think medication gets us to the point where we can start doing the effort. Like a jump-off.

David: You say 25 percent medication and you, Shawn, say only 5 percent. I guess the key point is both of you are not giving medication the entire credit.

Marlene: Right. Maybe it's close to only 15 percent.

David: This must suggest that Shawn possesses some real special abilities, since the changes were more effort than medication. Shawn, what skills do you have that helped you improve your concentration?

Shawn: I don't know.

David: Hmm . . . you don't like to brag about your talents? Do you mind if I say I'm impressed? I imagine your mother is, too.

Marlene: Oh, yeah! Shawn, I think is very smart and he never gives up.

David: So perseverance . . . never giving up is an anti-distraction technique?

Shawn: Yeah, I guess so.

David: I'm just thinking that lots of young people take Ritalin but don't put the effort in that you have. I think it must say something about your capabilities. Are you proud of yourself?

Shawn: Yes.

David: Why?

Shawn: Because I keep on trying, and I'm doing better in school.

This was my last meeting with Shawn. I awarded him a certificate (more on certificates and other documents to celebrate changes in Chapter Eight) as a Never Giver Upper.

———

The case examples in this chapter exemplify how SMART therapy expands on a sparkling moment to construct a compelling counterstory to ADHD. By entering the imaginary, the special abilities and knowledge of children labeled ADHD are articulated. Novel ideas and solutions emerge when we enter the unique worlds of children's imagination. Let's continue moving ahead and explore some creative ways to circulate the alternative story to a wider audience.

Chapter Eight

Step Five

Telling and Celebrating the New Story

After moving through the previous steps of the SMART approach, new stories have emerged and gained enough momentum to challenge the old ADHD story. However, it's difficult for new stories to survive if they are only told or heard in the therapy room. To help clients build on and solidify positive changes, the new story needs to be recognized by others, documented, and commemorated. This brings us to the fifth and final stage of SMART therapy: telling and celebrating the new story.

Step 5 ends therapy on a celebratory and joyful note—in contrast to the end of traditional therapy, when the client and therapist discuss termination issues such as grief and loss. In the SMART approach, therapy ends on a more upbeat note with an acknowledgment of the changes in the client's life. Telling and celebrating the changes includes one, some, or all of the following practices: (1) spreading the news by circulating the new story to a wider audience; (2) celebrating the changes through parties, certificates, and handbooks; (3) videotaping the final interview where the client is asked to be a consultant. This chapter will discuss these practices in detail.

Spreading the Good News

From a SMART perspective, new stories only take root in a child's life if there is an audience to appreciate them. If an alternative story is to gain substantial strength, notable developments and achievements must be circulated to concerned others: teachers, principals, friends, and family. As stated previously, in the absence of a strong, new story, the entrenched and deficit-saturated views of others can support the old ADHD story and undermine the child's progress. Thus it is imperative to document and distribute a revised and alternative story of the child. By widening the audience for the child's and family's achievements, the preferred story is further developed and authenticated.

Freedman and Combs (1996, p. 237) explain the appeal of spreading the news of preferred stories to significant others:

> Although in the dominant culture therapy tends to be a secret enterprise, in the narrative subculture the people who consult with us are usually enthusiastic about the idea of letting other people in on the process. We think that externalizing and antipathologizing practices offer people a different kind of experience in therapy. When therapy becomes a context in which people constitute preferred selves, they have nothing to hide, and much to show.

To return to the story of Huck Finn as an example, Huck's dominant story of being uncivilized and a poor lost lamb was supported by significant others in his life: the Widow Douglas, Miss Watson, Aunt Polly, Huck's teacher, Aunt Sally, and Judge Thatcher. Imagine yourself as Huck's SMART therapist if he were living today. As his therapist, you discover that he has an alternative story of heroism, fierce independence, creativity, bravery, and integrity. These qualities are dramatically documented in Huck's journey on the Mississippi, during which he saves the life of his friend and companion—the runaway slave, Jim.

Throughout the journey, Huck repeatedly protects and rescues Jim from those who seek to capture him and take him back to a life of slavery. Huck demonstrates cleverness and creative imagination on several occasions to keep Jim from being caught. These positive traits contradict the ADHD story, as Huck demonstrates an ability to achieve focus, make intelligent decisions, and show courage.

However, these qualities are mostly unknown or ignored by his community.

For the new story to take hold, all the important people in Huck's life need to be brought up to date with his positive achievements. Here are some ways to accomplish this:

- Ask Huck who knew he had these positive traits. He most likely would answer, "Jim." Ask what Jim saw in him that told him he had courage and integrity. Then ask, "If you were to see in yourself what Jim appreciated about you, what impact might this have on ADHD?" This question would help Huck appreciate himself through the eyes of another person.

- Invite Huck's significant others to a counseling session; include family members, teachers, and peers (especially Jim or Tom Sawyer).

- Draft a letter to Huck that records his achievements and circulates the news to his significant others.

- Co-write a news release that describes Huck's victories in a news headline format. Distribute this document to Huck's community.

- Have a ceremony during which Huck's achievements are recognized and celebrated. He could be awarded a certificate to honor his accomplishments.

- Encourage Huck to make an entry in an anti-ADHD handbook about his success. In this entry, Huck would offer advice to future readers (other children who are ADHD).

- Invite Huck to be interviewed on videotape about how he achieved what he did. This type of meeting is called a "consulting your consultant" interview (Epston and White, 1990, p. 25).

These methods of circulating the new story will be discussed in detail later in the chapter. For now, let's turn to questions we can ask our clients in order to identify and enlist an audience for positive developments.

Asking the Child for Help

The easiest way to recruit a wider audience for the preferred story is to ask the child for help. Ask who may need to be brought up to date with the changes. For example, the following questions can encourage children to name significant others who will help circulate the new story:

> Now that you have the upper hand on ADHD, who else would celebrate it with you? (Zimmerman and Dickerson, 1996).
>
> Who needs to be brought up to date with the changes you have been making?
>
> How could you let your teacher know that you are have improved your concentration abilities?
>
> Who in your life would have predicted that you could escape the effects of ADHD? What do they know about you that might have enabled them to predict this?
>
> If your grandmother (or other relative or friend) could be here with you now, what do you think she would say about your ability to conquer Boredom and ADHD?

These questions may encourage the child to initiate a conversation with the persons they have selected and recruited as an audience to the new story (Freedman and Combs, 1996). These conversations can be invaluable and empowering to the child, as they further amplify the new competency-based story. However, even if the child does not have the conversation with the person, a wider audience still develops in the child's thinking and imagination. The child is invited into an imaginary conversation in which she can have the experience of being appreciated and noticed by a wider audience and may evoke new awareness of her abilities and strengths. For example, Huck could be asked to imagine what Jim appreciated about his courage. Huck would then have viewed himself from Jim's eyes.

Inviting an Audience

Harlene Anderson and Harry Goolishian (1988) suggest that problems are maintained through language and social interaction. For example, when a young person is labeled ADHD, many systems may become involved in describing and directing the child's life (such as teachers, school counselors, probation officers, principals, and parents, among others), each with their own ideas, languages, values, and concerns. Anderson and Goolishian refer to these voices as problem-determined systems.

In order to address the effects of these voices on the child, SMART therapists often invite representatives of problem-determined systems into therapy meetings. Their presence allows the child to bring these important actors up to date with encouraging new developments and to invite more membership in an audience to honor and perform the child's current story.

Freedman and Combs (1996) explain the process of inviting others to a meeting:

> During that first phone call we introduce the possibility of everyone coming to the meeting. We appreciate the language "introduce the possibility" because a direct request for the presence of friends, relatives, co-workers, or representatives of involved agencies can be an occasion for distress. When most people originally seek therapy, the dominant discourses lead them to assume that something is wrong with them. If we suggest including other people in the process, they may imagine experiences of embarrassment, shame and possibly social control. As their assumptions about therapy are deconstructed in the course of our work together, people tend to be more open and even enthusiastic about inviting others to join in. The

final choice about who should attend the therapy meetings is, of course, always in the hands of the people who consult us [p. 240].

Case Example: Recruiting an Audience for Andrea

My work with Andrea, age nine, is an example of recruiting an audience to the new story. Andrea was labeled ADHD due to her problems with concentration, restlessness, temper outbursts, poor grades, and difficulty making and keeping friends. I worked with Andrea and her parents, Rob and Janet, over an extensive period. Rob and Janet were both dedicated to helping Andrea "beat Temper, Trouble, and ADHD" and attended all of Andrea's meetings. I often saw Andrea and her family in our reflecting team format.

Slowly but surely, with the team's help, Andrea began to make some small changes. For instance, her grades improved, she made a friend named Sarah, and she was able to calm her temper. To further amplify and celebrate these changes, I asked Andrea whom she might want to invite to a team session. These people would be able to join her team against ADHD—to add strength (in numbers) to her efforts to resist the problem. Andrea quickly suggested her friend Sarah. I also wondered if her teacher, Mr. Barker, would be a good team member. Andrea and her family found Mr. Barker to be very supportive of Andrea and said yes to my idea.

Sarah and Mr. Barker attended the next session. They sat in the room with Andrea, her family, and me and listened to our therapy conversation. The conversation focused on ways that Andrea was improving her focus and calming her temper. We invited Sarah and Mr. Barker to listen to our conversation and let them know that, at different points, we would ask them for their thoughts. Both Sarah and Mr. Barker added a great deal of information, which further increased Andrea's awareness of her successes and resources for support.

Sarah said that Andrea was a good friend. I asked Sarah to list all the qualities Andrea had that made her a good friend. On the board in the therapy room, she wrote the following:

- She shows caring by talking to me.
- She doesn't argue or blame me.
- She keeps promises.
- She can be trusted.
- She is a lot of fun!

These descriptions of Andrea contradicted the idea that she was incapable of making friends.

Mr. Barker added more to the new story by saying that he was noticing new developments also. To match what Sarah did, I asked him to list the changes he was noticing. Here is what Andrea's teacher listed on the board:

- She is participating in class discussion.
- She is asking questions when not understanding something.
- She is taking notes.
- She is completing her homework.
- She is breaking the daydreaming habit.
- She has been calming her Temper.

I asked Mr. Barker what these changes might mean for Andrea, and he said, "She is improving her ability to concentrate . . . she is maturing." I then inquired as to what it said about Andrea that she achieved these accomplishments. Mr. Barker replied, "She is an interesting, smart, and capable student."

I then turned to Andrea and asked her if she knew that others were seeing her in this way. She smiled and said, "No." I then asked Andrea what's it like that Mr. Barker and Sarah see these changes. Andrea replied, "It means everything to me . . . it's nice."

The changes that were discussed and highlighted helped Andrea to step further into the new story. The comments that Mr. Barker and Sarah made helped her maintain her new version of herself. As a result, Andrea's parents started noticing similar changes at home.

Sending Clients Letters

Letters are a great way to heighten an alternative story. The practice of letter writing is closely related to narrative therapy (White and Epston, 1990). Epston (1994) describes the reason for therapeutic letters:

> Conversation is by its very nature, ephemeral. After a particularly meaningful session, a client walks out aglow with some provocative new thought, but a few blocks away, the exact words that had stuck home as so profound may already be hard to recall. . . . But the words in a letter don't fade and disappear the way conversation does; they endure through time and space, bearing witness to the work of therapy and immortalizing it [p. 31].

The clients we work with find letters very useful; they help authenticate the new story. Many of my clients read and reread the letters, many times, long after therapy is ended. I conducted a survey of forty people I worked with to whom I had sent letters in the course of therapy. The results showed that one letter was worth 3.2 sessions of good, face-to-face therapy (Nylund and Thomas, 1994). Epston did a similar study and found that the average letter was worth 4.5 interviews.

SMART therapists take good notes during the therapy session and write the letter soon after the end of the meeting. The writing of the letter gives us the opportunity to reflect on the session. Often ideas come to us after the fact, and these ideas are included in the letter. The letters serve three central aims: (1) to summarize and recap our meetings, (2) to extend ideas or stories that were initiated in a therapeutic conversation, and (3) to include people who didn't attend a meeting.

In SMART therapy with children labeled ADHD, we ask the young person to whom they want the letter sent. Often the letters are circulated to relatives, friends, teachers, school counselors, and principals. The letter becomes another vehicle to disseminate new stories.

Letter to Adam

The following is an example of a letter David Epston (Epston, 1997, pp. 73–74) wrote to a young person, Adam, who had been diagnosed ADHD and was having problems with self-control. At school his peers teased him; they call him weird and different. Epston worked with Adam to appreciate his weird abilities. This letter (addressed to Adam and his mother, Sharon, and sister, Jenni) highlights Adam's recent successes at self-control:

Dear Adam:

You said that the last letter "had a good feeling." I am glad you thought so as I did too. And what was even better was that we continued to have a good conversation yesterday. I hope you felt that I was able to keep up with you at long last, although I may never get an "Irish sense of humor." In that regard, I may be a lost cause.

When I asked if you were able to make your self-control endure, you said that "it had switched on and off during the week." When I inquired as to how you understand what switched self-control off and on, you said that "tiredness and grumpy people switch off self-control" and "happiness and food switch on self-control."

Sharon, you added that "a great deal of physical activity" plays an important part in self-controlling ways. Sharon, you observed that when Adam is exercising his self-control, this has the effect of you experiencing him as "a good son and a good friend."

Adam, you seemed pleased to hear your mum say this. You then went on to tell me some things that were pretty new to me: "To a weirdly abled person with ADD, the tables are turned. Physical activity will wind up most normal people but in me physical activity will relax me and make me more self-controlling." Can you understand that wasn't immediately comprehensible to me? When I asked how long you had been aware of this, you said that "the theory has been there for the past 2, 3 years but I didn't know it was there."

Do you think we have hit upon something important if you are to have more of a self-controlling life and less of a life controlled by ADD? Does such a prospect appeal to you? Do you think it would appeal to your mum and Jenni?

Do you think you might develop an anti-ADD practice from the theory that you have had for the past 2, 3 years?

Would you do so by some inimitable "weirdly abled" ways and means?

Do you think I think you will come up with some predictable or unpredictable ways of making a self-controlling practice out of your "theory"?

What bearing might it have on your life if it became a more self-controlled life rather than an ADD-controlled life?

How would you try out such a practice in your life? Or would you prefer to surrender this lifetime to ADD and live your life out according to ADD?

We then got talking about your self-pride, something ADD has never been able to take away from you. Adam, can you imagine where you would be today if it had? I would hate to think about it. You put your self-pride down to yours and your family's "Irish sense of humor." Can you understand now why I have come to respect your "Irish sense of humor" so much more than when I first met you?

Still, you said that you had to "build up" your pride in the face of a lot of teasing. You considered that it was very advantageous that you had "a proud mother." When I asked you, Adam, what you were most proud of, you said, "At school, I have overcome the hurdle of teasing."

Sharon, you have undertaken quite a unique form of parenting, one that I expect plays quite a part in Adam's self-pride. You told me, "I have always challenged their minds. I was on my own for so long, I have always treated them as equals." And I understand that many people really don't respect you for having done this. Does that have to do with Adam and Jenni not being deferential to adults? Does that get them into trouble with some adults?

Merry Xmas and can we look forward to a more self-controlling 1996? I trust so.

David

Creating News Releases

Another method that helps to publicize the positive changes is the creative use of press releases. I began using them with Anthony, a young person who was interested in becoming a reporter. He was diagnosed with ADHD and was having problems completing his homework. We discussed how ADHD would "keep him from his newspaper career."

As the therapy progressed, Anthony progressed also. To promote these achievements we co-wrote a news headline and article that highlighted recent developments in Anthony's relationship with ADHD. Anthony and I felt compelled to let significant others know of his arrival at a "new status" in his life—one of being in control of ADHD. The news release was mailed out to his teacher and principal.

Case Example: Anthony's News Release

Anthony gets the upper hand on ADHD! He learns to conquer Boredom! Parents resign from the role of homework police!

Manteca, January 27, 1997

Anthony an 11-year-old from Manteca, California, has beaten back ADHD and Boredom! He was very much bossed around by the ADHD in the classroom and home. In class, he was struck by Boredom. Instead of listening to the teacher, Anthony found himself daydreaming or focus-ing on what was happening outside the classroom window. He had no idea what to say when the teacher called on him because his mind was else-where. His grades nose-dived below the ocean—below "C" level.

At home he was constantly reminded by his parents to do his home-work, which led to temper and arguing, which interfered in their relation-ship. His parents were frustrated, as they felt that they were recruited into the role of the homework police. ADHD had almost convinced Anthony that he was stupid or dumb.

To both the school's and his parents' surprise, Anthony decided to turn the corner on the ADHD. Recently, Anthony has conquered Bore-dom by using it as an opportunity to do something interesting. "Boredom is like when your brain gets hungry . . . it needs something to keep it alert." Anthony asked his teacher if he could sit in a different chair when Boredom attacked. This helped him to stay attentive. He also began to do imagination exercises—aerobics of the mind that helped Anthony to keep interested in what the teacher was saying. For instance, Anthony would pretend he was in the Wild West when his teacher gave a history lesson, or he would ask himself, "How would I explain this lesson to my dog, Yoshi?"

"When the teacher gives me some time for class-work and I would get frustrated, I now clinch my fist and count to 10 slowly. That will make you feel better," Anthony told Dave. He went on, "Try to block out everything for 10 seconds. Then try to listen harder and don't think you can't concentrate because you can!" These ideas helped Anthony get the upper hand on ADHD, and his grades are back up above the C level.

Anthony's parents are pleased with his comeback. "We no longer have to remind him of his homework . . . he reminds himself," Anthony's mother exclaimed. "We have escaped the conflict." Anthony now initi-ates his own homework. To keep Boredom from attacking during his homework, he takes a break every 20 minutes. Anthony works best in a quiet room so he can focus better.

"I now look at my homework as my work, not my parents' work. My parents don't have to yell at me anymore," Anthony proudly shared

with Dave. With these recent changes, ADHD doesn't stand a chance of taking control of Anthony!

Celebrating

SMART therapy is further influenced by White and Epston's ideas regarding the ending of therapy. Instead of viewing the end of therapy as termination or loss, Epston and White prefer a "rite of passage" metaphor (van Gennep, 1960). In this ritual process, a person is encouraged to "negotiate the passage from novice to veteran, from client to consultant. Rather than instituting a dependency on 'expert knowledge' presented by the therapist and authorities, this therapy enables persons to arrive at a point where they can take recourse to liberating and 'special knowledges' that they have resurrected and/or generated in therapy" (Freeman, Epston, and Lobovits, 1997, p. 126).

Employing this metaphor offers us the opportunity to celebrate the child's new status. We often invite the child and his community (family members, friends, and teachers) to attend a party at our clinic where the changes are reviewed. Often the child summarizes his own accomplishments, reads a poem, or shows his artwork. The ceremony is similar to a graduation, complete with food and festivities.

Ceremonies and Parties

A particularly memorable ceremony was the "Overcoming ADHD Party" for Chris. Chris, age nine, was referred to me by his teacher, Mrs. Baker, for problems with paying attention and being disorganized. With the help of his teacher, Chris was able to improve his concentration by sitting in the front of the room. Mrs. Baker and Chris came up with a prearranged signal (raising her left forefinger) to remind Chris to get back on track. Chris also cleaned up his messy desk and became better organized.

To commemorate these changes, Chris, his parents, and I threw a party at my clinic. Chris provided the cake and I brought drinks. Several of my colleagues were invited, as was Mrs. Baker.

At the party, Mrs. Baker and I shared our excitement at witnessing Chris's accomplishments. Chris then spoke about how he was able to listen better in class. "You just have to have a strong mind and tell ADHD and Boredom to not bother you," Chris advised the party attendees. He thanked Mrs. Baker and me for being on his team. I then awarded Chris with a certificate (see Figure 8.1). We all had fun.

Figure 8.1. Chris's Certificate.

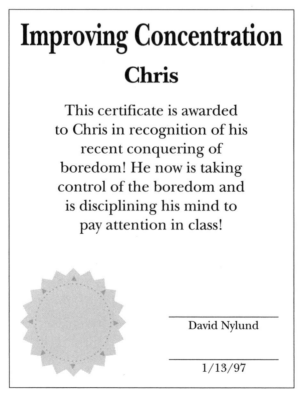

Improving Concentration

Chris

This certificate is awarded
to Chris in recognition of his
recent conquering of
boredom! He now is taking
control of the boredom and
is disciplining his mind to
pay attention in class!

David Nylund

1/13/97

Antiproblem Handbooks

Jenny Freeman has developed the practice of using antiproblem handbooks. Children are invited to make an entry in a handbook when they have had some success in conquering a problem. The handbooks (Freeman, Epston, and Lobovits, 1997) enable and honor children by inviting them to consult for the benefit of other children experiencing a comparable problem. Second, the handbooks serve to document their successes for reference and encouragement in case the client has a setback. Some examples of her handbook titles include *The Kid's Temper Tamer Handbook, The Fear Facer's and Worry Stopper's Handbook, Making Friends with Your Imagination*, and *The Freedom from Habits Handbook*.

Freeman, Epston, and Lobovits (1997) state:

> It is important to note that a handbook is not intended to be a record of those who are successful and experienced to be presented to those who are new and less competent. Neither is it intended to be used as a manual or guide. This in not in the spirit of the handbook. Nevertheless, children entering therapy can sometimes be offered stories about those who have traveled the road they are on. Children who are ready for such input from other children will show their readiness by their high interest level. However, we consider the main value of the handbooks to be the child's participation as he makes his own entry. Many children are so interested in being contributors that they don't even take the time to read the previous entries. When a child does read the entries of his predecessors, he is typically inspired to make his own contribution [pp. 136–137].

Inspired by Freeman, I have developed an Anti-ADHD Handbook. I've had experiences similar to hers: children are motivated and inspired to make an entry in the book. Here are a few entries:

> ADHD had a good friend in Temper. I overcame having tantrums by keeping myself entertained. I realized that I had Temper when I

was hungry or bored. I went bike riding or went in my room. I stated clearly when I went to my room, "Leave me alone, Temper!" When someone instigates me, I leave the scene. Also having friends kept me cool. (Melissa, age seven)

ADHD had me forgetting things all the time. I would lose things like homework and pencils. What helped to improve my memory is to write notes to myself on yellow stickpads. And I also got a remind myself calendar. You should do the same. (Seymour, age ten)

I had to try harder to concentrate. It was so hard! ADHD is very tricky! What helped was to participate in class discussions and ask questions a lot. I also looked at the teacher and zoned everything else out. I also sat next to a friend who had good concentration and studying habits! When I would do homework at home, I would take short breaks and get something to eat. I also pictured in my mind what I was reading so I could remember it better. (Billy, age fifteen)

There is even room for parents to make entries in the handbook. Thus, parents' own knowledge about how to deal with spirited children gets circulated to other parents. Here is an entry from a parent:

I wouldn't say it has been easy to live with a child influenced by ADHD. It is often challenging to see my 5-year-old son John's positive traits. However, it is important to focus on the positive aspects inherent in ADHD. This helps to reduce hopelessness. John is really gifted at music, sports and is very intuitive! I really compliment him on these talents and how he can use them to reduce ADHD's influence. In regards to John's unpleasant behaviors such as Temper, it is really important to set clear limits. I give John 5 minutes of time out when he has a tantrum. I also make eye contact with him so he clearly hears me. I also think it is important to spend a good hour each day alone with your child. John really calms down when I give him good attention. Don't give up and get discouraged! Your child has talents. (Stella, parent of ADHD child, John)

Videotaping a Final Interview

A great way to circulate the new story is to interview children on videotape (with signed consent) about how they were able to make the changes. I've mentioned before that Epston and White (1990) refer to this practice as consulting your consultant. Typically, this kind of interview is the final meeting between the child and the therapist. By enlisting children with ADHD as consultants on the problem, they assume a unique role (Freeman, Epston, and Lobovits, 1997, p. 126):

- They are consulted as authorities on their own lives.
- Their preexisting and newly acquired knowledge and abilities are deemed effective and worthy of respect.
- Their ideas are considered significant enough to be documented and circulated to others.

Children became quite honored and enthused about being interviewed on tape as an expert. By becoming experts in their own life, children become less dependent on expert knowledge. This can lead to more viable and enduring change.

Case Example: Julia Becomes the Expert

The following is a consulting-your-consultant interview I conducted with Julia, age nine. She was diagnosed with ADHD due to problems with inattention and hyperactivity. Julia was a bright, engaging, and playful child. We called the problem the Hyper Rascal. With a combination of expressive arts therapy and externalizing the problem, Sarah was able to improve her attention span and her behavior. She was very excited to be interviewed as a consultant. Here is that interview:

David: Why don't we start by you talking about what the Hyper Rascal was getting you to do?

Julia: I was getting into trouble.

David: What kind of trouble?

Julia: Like I would not pay attention to the teacher. I would pay attention to other people. And I wanted to get everybody else talking. And I just wanted to walk around the room [laughs].

David: You have so much energy. That is one of your best talents. But it seemed that the Hyper Rascal was using your energy against you and getting you into classroom habits that lead to Trouble. Is that right Julia?

Julia: Yes.

David: What other ways was the Hyper Rascal trying to ruin you?

Julia: It was disturbing my concentration. I was forgetting what I should do for class work.

David: So it was taking over your concentration abilities?

Julia: Yes, it wanted me to concentrate on everything else but the teacher!

David: How about at home? How was the Hyper Rascal getting you there?

Julia: I wouldn't listen to my mom.

David: You wouldn't listen to your mom. Were you listening to the Hyper Rascal instead?

Julia: Yes.

David: What did the Hyper Rascal want you to do instead of listening to your mother?

Julia: It wanted me to just ignore her and just jump up and down on the couch!

David: And did you?

Julia: Oh yes [laughs].

David: Could you show me what the Hyper Rascal did to you and your body?

Julia: OK [Julia laughs and then stands up on the couch in my room and jumps up and down].

David: Wow. It could really make you hyper!

Julia: [Sits back down] Yes!

David: So sometimes the Hyper Rascal would get you to be wiggly and squirmy inside?

Julia: Yes, like an earthworm.

David: Yeah that's good! Like an earthworm. So the Hyper Rascal gets kids to act like earthworms?

Julia: Yes. It would just take me over and I couldn't stop it!

David: So would you say the Hyper Rascal was more of an enemy or a friend to you?

Julia: More of an enemy.

David: Why was it an enemy?

Julia: Because it was getting me in trouble.

David: Was it stealing your maturity?

Julia: Yes. It would make me act like a four-year-old.

David: So the Hyper Rascal was definitely in charge of you. How did you start to take your life back from the Hyper Rascal?

Julia: By drawing pictures of the Hyper Rascal and seeing it as a person who was bothering me. I then told it to stop bothering me and get out!

David: What happened then?

Julia: I still squirmed a little but I started to calm down and concentrate.

David: How did you do that? I am asking this because other kids who are bothered by Hyper Rascal are going to watch this tape and get some good advice from you.

Julia: Well, I just worked really, really hard at paying attention and not listening to anybody else but the teacher.

David: Anything else, Julia? Let's say I am working with a kid whose mind and body is bothered by Hyper Rascal. What can they do to get rid of it?

Julia: They can take a chill pill!

David: What's a chill pill?

Julia: It's like your own pill. You have another pill and that pill's the bad pill. But you also have a good pill inside you. So you try to fight that bad pill off. It's hard but you can do it. I am trying to demonstrate right now by sitting still and listening to you. I can be a magician you know!

David: How so? What magic can you perform?

Julia: I am showing my powers of concentration.

David: And you're doing a good job! So you have to take your mind back from the Hyper Rascal by using magic? Would you say that you are getting stronger and the Hyper Rascal is getting weaker?

Julia: Yes.

David: Now that you are not at the mercy of the Hyper Rascal, what do you know about yourself that you can appreciate?

Julia: I feel that I can do anything! Goodbye Hyper Rascal! [waves goodbye]

David: Any parting words of advice for the young people who will watch this tape?

Julia: Don't fall for it! Don't fall for that icky, yucky, dirty, dumpy Hyper Rascal!

David: What do you see for your future now?

Julia: I can concentrate now. I have lots of friends now. I can see a good future.

David: Thanks Julia. You have given some very good advice. Thanks a lot.

This chapter illustrates the fifth and final stage of the SMART approach. Instead of the final stage of therapy being informed by the "termination as loss" metaphor, we view the ending phase as one of celebration and acknowledgment. The child's own knowledge about solutions is privileged and circulated to a wider audience. This practice makes therapy playful and helps consolidate and sustain the preferred story.

Chapter Nine

Putting It All Together

SMART Therapy from Beginning to End

In previous chapters I introduced each of the five steps of SMART therapy. I described my intentions in each step and the methods I use to work with children and parents to deconstruct old, limiting stories and build new, empowering stories. Although I described the steps in a linear fashion, like any good adventure SMART therapy is not usually a linear process. Many of the steps overlap, and therapy can take a number of exciting turns that challenge us, as clinicians, to revisit and refine our work.

At this juncture in our journey, let's explore a case vignette that demonstrates how I used the SMART approach from start to finish with one client, Jeremy—a spirited boy who, based on his Huck-like qualities, had been diagnosed with ADHD. In this example I demonstrate each of the steps in SMART therapy, and you may notice how the steps overlap and emerge in a different order as Jeremy, his parents, and I take on the Monsters.

Case Example: Jeremy Is Done with the Monster

Jeremy, age eight, was referred to me by his pediatrician because of persistent temper tantrums, overactivity, and difficulty concentrating. Dr. Johnson had recently prescribed Ritalin for Jeremy after having diagnosed him with ADHD. Jeremy was the second-oldest

---

A portion of this chapter first appeared in 1994 in *The Journal of Collaborative Therapies*. Reprinted with permission.

of four boys. His older brother, Michael, was also ADHD and had been taking Ritalin for over a year.

First Session

Jeremy came to the first session with his parents, Jan and Steve. The parents described the problems as "Jeremy's attention-deficit problems" and "his attitude." They were particularly concerned with Jeremy's frequent tantrums and his fighting with Michael. Jan showed me Jeremy's recent school reports, which were not flattering. The teacher described his problems with staying on task and his lack of concentration. Steve felt that Jeremy was "turning out just like Michael."

While talking to Jan and Steve, Jeremy stared out my window as if he was not listening to our conversation. I attempted to gain his attention by talking about externalizing the problem (step 1). I asked Jeremy to name the problem in his own words. Soon Jeremy became more engaged in the discussion and named the problems that were affecting his life the Temper Monster and the Hyper Monster.

I questioned Jeremy on how the Hyper Monster and the Temper Monster were influencing him (step 2). These questions included the following:

Do they gang up on you, Jeremy? Do they like trouble?

What do they get you to do?

What classroom habits does the Hyper Monster like you to do?

Have the monsters taken away your talents? Are there any talents left for Jeremy?

What are the monsters doing to your parents?

In response to these effects questions, Jeremy felt that the monsters were his enemy and were keeping him from paying attention to his teacher and parents. He agreed that the Hyper Monster had "stolen his concentration from him" and was getting him in trouble at school. Jeremy also began to discover that the Temper Monster was getting him to "act before thinking."

As this externalizing conversation continued, Jan and Steve informed me of Jeremy's talents, while Jeremy commented that he couldn't think of anything he was good at. I began to focus my attention on some of Jeremy's forgotten abilities (step 4). Jan reminded Jeremy of his abilities in art and athletics. In fact, Jeremy had written and illustrated a book for school and received first place in the contest! He also was a star baseball and football player. I asked Jeremy to explain these exceptions (step 3):

How do you say No! to the Hyper Monster and concentrate on art?

So you are able to use your extra energy for baseball and football.
   How do you do that?

Jeremy appeared to be delighted to make the Hyper Monster mad. I speculated with Jeremy and his parents about what might happen if Jeremy used his concentration and athletic abilities for his benefit rather than let the Hyper Monster steal them.

Letter to Jeremy

By the end of their first session Jeremy and his parents were clearly united to weaken the Hyper Monster. Because Jeremy was interested in athletics, he used metaphors of "winning over" and "defeating" the Hyper Monster. I then inquired if Jeremy was ready to "go to work against both of the Monsters." Jeremy said he was eager to take his life back from the "terrible duo." I summarized the first session with a letter that I faxed to Jeremy and his parents:

Dear Jeremy:

The Hyper Monster and its friend, the Temper Monster, were stealing your talents from you. Jeremy, the monsters were ganging up on you and getting you in trouble both at school and at home. The Temper Monster has been really tricky at getting you to fight with Michael. The monsters also have made your parents worry about you. Your parents were tricked by the monsters into thinking that you were too weakened to make a comeback.

However, I bet the Hyper Monster was mad to find out that you can sit still and do your artwork. I bet it was also very angry when you talked to me about your talents at sports. Your parents are proud of you and your talents. They are on your side against the monster. Boy, I bet the Hyper Monster is having a temper tantrum, now!

Jeremy, you told me that you were ready to defeat the Hyper Monster. To beat up on the monster you agreed to do the following:

- You are to write and illustrate a book about your defeat of the monster.
- You will spend some time each day strengthening your concentration by timing yourself on how long you can stay focused on your homework.
- You thought it would be a good idea to sit in the front of the classroom to pay attention to the teacher.

Jeremy, do you think you'll enjoy getting over on the monster by doing those three anti-hyper assignments? Your parents agreed to help you. Good luck!

> Yours against the monster,
> David Nylund
> P.S. Jeremy, please show this letter to your parents!

Second Session

In the next session, Jeremy enthusiastically told me about his recent successes in school and at home (step 3). Jan shared that Jeremy's attention span was improving, both at home and at school (according to Jeremy's teacher, with whom I conferred throughout the therapy). He was also becoming more organized, had no tantrums, and was following directions better.

Despite these successes, Jan expressed some resignation about Jeremy's future because he was ADHD. She wondered if some of the interventions in the therapy would really make a difference with Jeremy in the long run because (she said) ADHD is a long-term illness. She also wondered if Jeremy's recent changes were due solely to the medication. I invited Jan into a discussion about her understanding of ADHD (step 2). This led me to ask some deconstructing questions (adapted from Stewart and Nodrick, 1990):

Where did you get the idea that ADHD is an illness?

Does viewing it as an illness contribute to your pessimism?

Do you think that some people feel that individuals diagnosed as ADHD are flawed and have to settle for less in life?

What might happen to Jeremy if he felt that being diagnosed meant he was damaged or broken?

What message might Jeremy receive if he felt that Ritalin was totally responsible for his recent successes? How could both Jeremy and the medication be acknowledged?

In viewing your son as ADHD, how do you find yourself interacting with him? How does it affect your expectations of Jeremy?

How has the way in which Dr. Johnson (Jeremy's pediatrician) assessed and labeled your son influenced the life of the problem?

Do you think it is possible for a professional to truly determine the diagnosis of ADHD?

Your son, Michael, is diagnosed with ADHD for over a year. How has that influenced the way you view Jeremy?

My intent in asking those questions was to encourage multiple meanings of ADHD rather than simply to promote another expert view. I asked each question with genuine curiosity, and there was no single, correct answer I was looking for.

By reflecting on these questions, Jan reconsidered some of her ideas about ADHD. She agreed that it is probably not possible for any professional to make a definitive diagnosis. She decided that talking about the problem in a way Jeremy could relate to (the Hyper Monster) was more effective than discussing the problem from a more psychiatric or clinical viewpoint. Jan also wondered if Michael's problems were shaping the way she viewed Jeremy. She vowed to separate Michael's situation from Jeremy. Last, Jan no longer credited Ritalin as the sole impetus for Jeremy's recent changes.

Next, I asked Jeremy a series of landscape-of-action and landscape-of-meaning questions (step 4) to bring forth his personal agency. These questions included the following:

Jeremy, how did you improve your concentration?

What abilities are you using now to defeat the monsters?

Why are the monsters worried? What do you think they say, now that you have them on the run?

Jeremy said he was "listening to his parents better" by making eye contact and "telling the monsters to get out of my mind." He also had invented a special friend and protector to help him defeat the Hyper and Temper Monsters, Bekdo. Jeremy's imagination and creativity was very evident as he drew and described Bekdo as a fire fighter who puts out "temper fires."

Course of Treatment

Subsequent sessions built on Jeremy's successes over the monsters by using his imagination. Occasionally, setbacks would occur, particularly related to Jeremy's temper. I framed these setbacks as hiccups and opportunities for Jeremy to "show Temper who's boss." I asked a series of effects questions to help Jan and Steve recognize their inadvertent participation in the life support system of the Temper Monster (step 2). Both parents realized that the Monster relies on their giving too much attention to a tantrum. Exceptions were explored when Jan and Steve tuned the tantrums out and thus weakened the Temper Monster's influence.

The rules of the Hyper Monster were introduced in the third session (Stewart and Nodrick, 1990). A colleague of mine interviewed me as the Hyper Monster (step 1). While playing my role as the Hyper Monster, I was asked what strengthens me and what weakens me. Through a collaborative effort we came up with the "Rules of the Hyper Monster." They were as follows:

- The Monster (and his friend, the Temper Monster) depends on people hoping for a quick fix.
- The Monster is strengthened by pessimism and resignation.
- The Monster wants to blind children's parents to the young person's talents.
- The Monster is weakened by determination and humor.
- The Monster is weakened by attention to small successes.

Jan and Steve said these rules helped them pay attention to Jeremy's victories over the monsters. Jeremy and I faxed many messages to each other between sessions. The following are some of our many notes:

Dear Mr. Nylund:
I hope you are doing good. I like you a really lot. Guess what I'm doing? I'm doing my homework. The monsters don't stand a chance.
Happy Easter!
I was reading your letters and felt like writing you a letter.
      Have a good day!
      Jeremy

I then sent him a return note:

Dear Jeremy:
I received your fax . . . thanks. How are you doing? Have you finally slain the Hyper and Temper Monsters? Is Bekdo helping you? How's the book going? Did you have a good Easter?
David

Occasionally I sent Jeremy a fax from the Hyper Monster himself!

Hey Jeremy,
I heard you are faxing Mr. Nylund notes. You told him that you were beating me and my friend, the Temper Monster. I don't give up easily . . . you better be on guard with Bekdo! I would love it if you did not listen to your teacher's directions or if you did not strengthen your concentration. I'd really love it if you had a tantrum!
The Hyper Monster

I saw Jeremy and his parents for a total of five sessions over a five-month period. Jeremy brought a copy of his book, *Jeremy Is Done with the Monster*, to our fifth session. In this book, Jeremy shared his knowledge and expertise on how he overcame hyperactivity and temper tantrums. I told Jeremy his book was placed in the Anti-ADHD Archives so that other children could gain from his expertise (step 5).

Jeremy's idea about being done with the Hyper Monster meant that the monster was no longer his enemy but a friend. Because Jeremy was self-managing his own thinking and behavior, the former monster's tricks and tactics (excessive energy, distractibility) could now be used at Jeremy's convenience and for his benefit. He had redefined his relationship with the Hyper Monster. Jan and Steve reported that Jeremy's tantrums had significantly decreased. He also increased his ability to pay attention, follow directions, and listen better. I sent letters to his pediatrician and teacher that documented Jeremy's changes. These important people in Jeremy's life were thus recruited as a wider audience to his progress (step 5).

What impressed me (and his parents) the most was Jeremy's ability to generate his own solutions once he was taken seriously and the problem was framed in his own language. During a follow-up phone interview four months after the last session, Jeremy's parents reported that he continued to do well (with occasional hiccups), both at home and at school.

Chapter Ten

Huck at School

SMART Strategies in the Classroom

Never let school interfere with your education.
—*Mark Twain*

No book on the subject of treating ADHD would be complete without a discussion of schools and teaching, so let's turn our attention to the classroom. Huck Finn said he hated school. He found the emphasis on sitting still, memorizing, doing monotonous drills, reading, and writing to be humdrum in comparison to being free in the wilderness, rafting down the Mississippi. School did not capture his curiosity and imagination.

Imagine Huck in a classroom today. Would the learning process be any more exciting for him than it was in nineteenth-century Missouri? Or would it be similar? My guess is that Huck would find today's school to be just as uninspiring and restrictive—perhaps even more so because of larger and more impersonal classrooms and increased pressures and homework demands. Huck would no doubt be an excellent candidate for the ADHD label.

In today's typical classroom, Huck would spend several hours a day sitting quietly in class, listening to a great deal of verbal information from the teacher. He would complete countless workbooks and read extensively from dry and often outdated textbooks. In most classrooms, he would not have the opportunity to be engaged by his teacher or the material in a manner that would appeal to his learning style and imagination. In addition, because recess and creative classes such as art and music have been cut to make more time for math and reading, Huck would find himself without relief from the rigors of traditional academic instruction. Huck would most likely respond with fidgeting, hyperactivity, restlessness, and inattentiveness—in short, the classic symptoms of so-called ADHD.

Today's U.S. school system was patterned after German schools, which were developed in the 1800s for the specific aim of producing obedient soldiers and factory workers (Gallagher, 1999). Our schools operate much like those in Huck's day. Back then, creativity and independent thought and action were discouraged because such characteristics were viewed as problematic in a war or factory (Gallagher, 1999). Similarly, these traits clash with our modern, cookie-cutter educational system.

Clearly, children who behave in such a way that they might be labeled ADHD have difficulty with a restrictive educational system—one that emphasizes repetitive drills and memorization. To place a child on Ritalin so that he can succeed in this environment ignores the wider problem: the structure, tools, methods, and resources of our schools.

A child's imagination and willingness to learn are not harnessed in our traditional schools. Rather, there is an increasing tendency to adopt standardized testing in order to raise the public perception that schools are performing their function well. However, public opinion differs widely with regard to the function of modern schools. Should they focus on basic skills or critical thinking? What about citizenship and values?

As the debate rages over what schools should focus on, politicians, parents' associations, and school administrators have increasingly come to rely on standardized tests in an attempt to find some measure of school performance. Standardized test scores have been linked to school district funding and teacher pay increases. As a result, raising test scores has become of primary interest for educators. To raise test scores, children are asked to do lots of tedious homework, particularly in the areas of math and reading, to the exclusion of other activities, academic and creative subjects, or alternative learning approaches.

What are the effects of our current direction in education? One is that students assume a passive role in their own learning. The trend toward less recess and more homework makes learning dull for huge numbers of children. Creative and weirdly able children often have autonomous and idiosyncratic learning styles that are incongruous with the conventional system. When such a child acts up or gets distracted due to this incompatibility, he is often labeled ADHD.

What is the solution to this problem? I believe that the SMART principles can be adapted to fit the classroom. Teachers can use the guiding assumptions of SMART therapy to help harness the special abilities and talents of so-called ADHD kids. Let us examine the features of a SMART classroom, along with educational alternatives to the traditional classroom. Included is a discussion of practical classroom management and teaching strategies that honor and use ADHD children's unique strengths.

The SMART Classroom

The classroom environment must facilitate learning. The ideas I offer here for setting up such a classroom derive from my interviews with teachers and families about what works. First, the SMART classroom needs to be well organized; it works best if uncluttered. With children who have different learning styles and are likely to be labeled ADHD, it is beneficial to have clear structure and few outside distractions. It may be useful to have children who exhibit ADHD-like behaviors to sit away from diversions such as windows, doors, and pencil sharpeners.

How the classroom space is arranged is critical in increasing motivation and interest. To encourage group discussion, healthy interaction, and cooperative learning, desks should be grouped so that everyone can see each other. The traditional format (rows facing the teacher) suggests that all knowledge comes from the teacher, and students are passive recipients. As the children quoted in this book have shown us, passivity and boredom lead to ADHD attacks. Last, it is important to allow students to stand or walk around as they listen or work. Many children use their bodies to make sense of the subject. These active (kinesthetic) learners can become frustrated when they must sit still for long periods of time. They should not be punished for standing or moving around as long as they are not disruptive.

Now let's move ahead to classroom management and teaching strategies. I want to stress that the ideas to follow are not intended as criticism of teachers. Teachers face tremendous obstacles, including decreased funding and increased demands for efficiency and effectiveness, reduced support from parents, and increasingly challenging children. The following suggestions and case examples are offered as additions to a teacher's repertoire rather than replacements for what's already there.

The three features of SMART teaching are (1) solution-focused therapy, (2) multiple intelligence theory, and (3) critical pedagogy. I'll discuss each in detail.

Using Solution-Focused Principles

Solution-focused principles can easily be adopted in an educational context. Linda Metcalf (1999), a consultant to schools, has discussed how solution-focused ideas give teachers positive strategies for creating a positive and productive classroom in which each becomes responsible for his or her own actions.

The following is a list of ideas for working with students from a solution-focused perspective (Metcalf, 1999, p. 236):

- Talk about students with a nonpathological approach. Describe their difficulties in a more positive way to make their problem solvable.
- Do not worry about trying to figure out why a student is having a problem. Instead, watch for times when the problem is not there so much.

- See students as people who are stuck in a problem but are not themselves the problem. This will make it easier to help them escape.

- When a student has a problem, ask what he or she wants to be different.

- Remember, when you change your strategy, students change behaviors.

- Complex problems do not always call for complex solutions. Sometimes it just means we have to find problem-free times and learn what is different then.

- When we step into our students' lives and try to understand where they are, we will have less resistance.

- Motivation is necessary for change. Look for alternative, more positive ways to motivate students. Ask students what motivates them to learn.

- If a lesson plan works, do it. If a lesson plan does not work, don't do it again. The same principle applies to behavioral interventions. Do something different!

- Always focus on the possible and changeable when working with a student or parent. This will result in a solid goal that is achievable.

- Go slowly to build successes. Think of making a slight change, not a big one.

- Remember, rapid change can and does happen. Watch for changes and verbalize the changes to your students. Always ask them how they made even the smallest change.

- Change is constant. It will always happen when we do things differently.

- Always watch for "exceptions" to the problem. Notice what you are doing that helps exceptions happen. Notice what a student or a parent does.

- Change the time and the place so problems can't happen as they did before.
- See problems differently, as entities that influence a student but are *not* the student.

As you can see, these ideas are congruent with the SMART model and can be useful in working with children labeled ADHD. As stated earlier, a child so labeled can develop a deficit-saturated reputation. This reputation can recruit teachers into noticing the child only when the problem is occurring. ADHD students are often told what they are doing wrong, not what they do right, and this problem talk can be contagious. Students with ADHD can begin to believe that they cannot manage their own behavior. As a result, teachers feel that they need to be expert in managing children's behavior by using behavior modification.

The Trouble with Behavioral Modification

Behavior modification strategies are popular with teachers. These strategies can be effective in managing classroom behavior and academic performance because they focus on the positive efforts children make to change their behavior. However, this approach makes the teacher the expert, not the student. From this traditional approach, the personal agency of the child is not emphasized.

Osenton and Change (1999) write:

> While other models proceeding from a social learning or operant conditioning perspective have proposed the idea of "catch them doing good," a solution orientation is different in that an element of personal agency ("How did you do that?") is introduced, as opposed to merely receiving information. Children are seen not as merely responding to stimuli, but having their own competence enhanced [pp. 72–73].

For children who are labeled ADHD, behavior modification techniques can inadvertently reinforce the idea that the solution to their problem lies outside them. The solution is seen as some external stimulation such as Ritalin. Consequently, children turn the problem over to an expert to manage. The expertise of the teacher becomes privileged over the child's own knowledge.

Metcalf (1999) writes:

> The solution-focused teacher approaches problems differently . . . with a desire to look at her student's competencies instead of his deficits. She does not solve problems for students or parents; she lets the student's competencies guide her to solutions. She sees her task as helping the student identify his abilities through observations. In fact, his abilities are all that she looks for; she does not mention the deficits. This approach lends itself to a more collaborative relationship that often results in a student feeling as if the teacher is on his side. What makes it different from a purely behavior modification approach is that the teacher does not compliment just when the student does well, as if only to praise or reinforce him, she compliments the student from a stance of amazement, curiosity, and discovery [p. 5].

Solution-focused ideas in the classroom help reverse the deficit logic and personal enfeeblement that is so often associated with ADHD. To help teachers develop solution-focused strategies, Metcalf has designed a worksheet. The questions in the worksheet help teachers generate solution-oriented conversations with ADHD children. Here are the questions (Metcalf, 1999, p. 11):

What is my goal in working with this student?

When in this class has the student responded effectively?

When else has the student shown the ability to make passing grades? How often, which assignments did he or she pass, and what do the student's successes tell about his or her abilities?

How can I share my discoveries of the student's successes effectively, so that he or she hears the successes and is motivated by them? How can I assist the student in rediscovering his or her successes personally?

How can this process begin on a small scale so that the student will be successful?

Using SMART and Solution-Focused Ideas

Let's turn to some case examples of using SMART, solution-focused ideas in the classroom. The SMART teacher uses a nonpathological approach by externalizing the problem. The first case (from Metcalf, [1999]) illustrates this with a student, Jon, labeled ADHD.

Case Example: Separating the Problem

The teacher named Jon's problem Energy. Jon was having problems completing his assignments. The teacher approached Jon in this way: "Jon, the Energy is keeping you from doing your worksheet. I noticed when you sat alone this morning at the table near the center, you completed your sentences. Where would you suggest going now so that you can finish this assignment?" (p. 14).

By using externalizing language, the perception of the problem changes. The teacher suggests that Energy is an entity outside of Jon and that he can control it. The conversation also implies that Jon will complete his worksheet. Even if Jon is a pupil who rarely finishes his assignments, talking to him in a solution-focused way will give him a different image of himself. Energy is the problem, not Jon. This can empower and motivate Jon to work harder at accomplishing his class work.

Looking for Exceptions

Metcalf encourages teachers to look for instances when the problem is less of a problem. She describes a teacher who was frustrated yet determined in her work with Sally, age ten.

Case Example: Solution-Oriented Therapy

Sally had refused to turn in her homework. Using traditional behavior modification techniques made little impact, as all conversations were problem-focused. After consultation with Metcalf (1999), the teacher decided to be solution-oriented in her conversation with Sally.

> *Teacher:* Sally, thanks for staying after class today. You know, I've been looking at my grade book, and do you realize that you have turned in seven of the last ten homework assuagements?
>
> *Sally:* No, I didn't.
>
> *Teacher:* That says a lot about you, Sally. It's now December, and when I looked back to the first of the year, I noticed that you had turned in all of the assignments except for only a few in the first three months. Your grades were high. You are such a good student. I am quite impressed with your past record.
>
> *Sally:* [silent but appears curious]
>
> *Teacher:* I'm a little sad for you, though, because when you forget to turn in your homework sometimes, your grades don't show what a good student you really are. I wonder, what is different on the days you do turn in the homework?
>
> *Sally:* Sometimes I write down the assignments and then I remember to do them at home. Sometimes I forget to write them down in class so I can't do them.

Teacher: According to my grade book, you turned in almost all of your assignments early in the fall. How did you remember then to write down the assignments?

Sally: [Thinking for a few minutes] I think it was when I sat next to the blackboard where you always wrote down the assignments. I always copied them when you reminded us to do it before school ended.

Teacher: Are you saying that sitting next to the board helped that much . . . and that my reminding you helped?

Sally: I guess so. In my music class I always remember to practice my flute because the teacher gives us practice sheets for our parents to sign. I have it every day. I guess I need reminders and to see it written down.

Teacher: What do you think you might do for the next few days to help you remember? I'm interested in helping you get back on track like you were before. It must have been fun for you to show everyone what a good student you were.

Sally: Yes. My mom was happy then. Maybe I could sit up close to the board again?

Teacher: I'll be glad to let you sit close again. Over the next few days I will be looking forward to seeing you turn in your homework like you used to. I will be glad to remind you to write things down as well. Could you write me a note to keep here on my desk so I don't forget? [pp. 98–99].

This conversation implied that Sally was capable of turning in her homework. Instead of making suggestions to Sally, the teacher placed her in the expert role by asking her what had worked in the past and giving her all the credit. This focus on exceptions brought forth a dialogue of possibility. Sally's teacher said she would look for future exceptions—times when Sally did her homework. This set the stage for Sally to find her own intrinsic motivation. She began completing her homework, and her grades improved significantly.

Solution-Focused Classroom Management

Tanya Osenton and Jeff Chang (1999) describe using solution-oriented ideas to manage the classroom. They developed and piloted the plan in a first grade classroom in Calgary, Alberta, Canada. Many of the children were viewed as having "high needs" such as ADHD or other behavior disorders.

Instead of laying down rules autocratically, Osenton and Chang used a democratic approach. On the first day of class, the teacher asked the students a version of the miracle question: "Imagine that tonight, after we all have gone home, a miracle happens, and tomorrow when we come back to school, we have the perfect classroom environment. What will be different? What will be the same? How will we know a miracle has occurred?" (Osenton and Chang, 1999, p. 70). This question generated a lively dialogue on the image of an ideal classroom. Students discussed the ideal class as a place to "learn new things, meet new friends, be safe and have fun" (p. 70). Prompted by these ideas, the students generated the classroom rules collaboratively. These rules were displayed on a huge bulletin board that was colorful and visually appealing.

The students were then asked to track and note instances in which the miracle was happening. The students became very invested in watching for exceptions and noting when the hypothetical solution was occurring. At the end of each day, the students were asked to rate the class using a scaling question (Berg and Miller, 1992), with 1 denoting a very bad day and 10 indicating the miracle.

The solution-oriented approach helped the teacher move out of the expert role as she listened to the expertise of her students. This democratic process encouraged the first graders to become actively invested in positive outcomes. Students became adept at noticing exceptions of their peers and asking landscape-of-action questions. The classroom become a "community of concern" (Madigan and Epston, 1995, p. 257) in which solutions, competency, and personal agency were generated and appreciated.

One idea that SMART teacher Scott Clary (personal communication, 1999) used to create a community of concern was that of "study buddies." He used this approach with Rajiv, a fourth grader who was very active and distractible. Scott paired him with a calmer student, Derek, who had good study habits. Derek helped Rajiv stay on track when he became diverted from his work. As Rajiv's attention span improved, Derek was able to monitor and note his progress. Together, the two students were able to accomplish what Rajiv could not have accomplished alone.

The SMART classroom includes these solution-focused ideas because they help ADHD children notice their special abilities and personal agency. By including children labeled ADHD in a democratic and collective process regarding the rules and classroom environment, their knowledge is valued. This counters the school experience of many ADHD kids who feel that teachers and school personnel disregard them.

Multiple Intelligence Theory

Harvard researcher Howard Gardner (1983) wrote a popular book called *Frames of Mind* that refutes the commonly accepted idea that people are born with a fixed and singular type of intelligence that can only be discovered by IQ tests. Instead, Gardner says there are at least seven types of intelligences. These include linguistic, mathematical, spatial, kinesthetic, musical, interpersonal, and intrapersonal intelligences.

Gardner states that most schools focus only on linguistic and logical-mathematical skills (reading, writing, math, and science) and ignore the other five intelligences. Children who possess high levels of the other five intelligences but who have difficulty in the linguistic and logical areas may be at risk for being labeled. Often these children end up feeling incompetent because they are always struggling in school. For example, a child who learns by moving around and is good at athletics (bodily-kinesthetic intelligence) has difficulty sitting still in a classroom and completing linguistic and mathematical materials. He is at special risk for the ADHD label, as his energy and physical intelligence will be pathologized as hyperactivity and impulsivity.

The solution, according to Gardner, is to create classrooms that teach and honor all seven intelligences. Thomas Armstrong (1995) suggests:

> If our nation's classrooms taught more often in this multiple-intelligences way, we'd have fewer students identified as ADD. Students would have frequent experiences of being taught in the way they most easily learn. The strongly bodily-kinesthetic child would be able to channel much of his distractible, hyperactive, impulsive behavior into physical experiences that are academically rewarding. Similarly, highly musical, social, spatial or intrapersonal students would be able to show their strengths frequently in the classroom and would have less need to "act out" the intelligences inappropriately [pp. 95–96].

A SMART classroom actively uses the multiple intelligence (MI) approach to teaching. The classroom becomes a vehicle for students to embrace their own learning style and shine. When MI is used, the classroom becomes more experiential and hands-on.

The following is an example of using MI with a student, Andy, who was labeled ADHD.

Case Example: Andy Gets the Rap on Math

Andy, age eleven, was in Irene Borrego's (personal communication, 1999) fifth grade class. (Irene currently is a multiple intelligence specialist who consults to schools using MI.) Early in the year, she taught the students about MI theory by using a visual aid—a picture of a pizza. The pizza had seven slices on it. Each slice represented one of the seven intelligences that Gardner talks about.

Students were asked to pick their strongest slice (area) of intelligence and their weakest slice. Andy, who had problems with attention span, picked musical as his best intelligence. He loved rap music. Logical-mathematical was his weakest link. However, Andy was interested in math because he wanted to improve his multiplication skills.

Irene's assessment showed that he knew the multiplication tables only through the 5's. Using MI theory, Irene asked Andy how he might use his strongest link (music) to aid his weakest link (math). He quickly came up with the idea of making a math rap tape. Andy completed the tape right away, and soon he had learned the multiplication tables through 12. The rap tape was then placed at the math center for other students to use. Andy had become a consultant to other students who were struggling with math (similar to step 5 of the SMART model).

Andy continued to struggle with his attention span, but he improved when given the opportunity to learn the subject matter on his own. By having others acknowledge and accept his ideas for learning, Andy transitioned from a passive to an active learner. And we know that ADHD hates active learners!

Critical Pedagogy

SMART teaching has been strongly influenced by Brazilian educator, Paulo Freire. Freire and his colleagues (hooks, 1994; Giroux, 1992; Shor, 1992) deconstruct and critique the traditional educational system; they encourage their students to be active learners, cultural resisters, and critical thinkers—a type of teaching called critical pedagogy.

Freire refers to the conventional approach to teaching as the "banking model" (Freire, 1970. p. 12). The banking system of education refers to the idea that teachers are like bankers—the experts who make deposits of information and knowledge into the empty accounts of students. Students are encouraged to memorize the information (mostly math and reading) and demonstrate their understanding of it by scoring high on so-called objective tests.

Banking education assumes that the teacher is the expert and the student is a passive, one-way recipient of the teacher's information. The teacher chooses the program content (because the teacher alone determines what is important and what is unimportant for students to learn), and students are forced to adapt to the teacher's ideas. This one-way process of education places students in a passive role. Students are not engaged in critical thinking, rather, they are spoon fed what someone else thinks they ought to be interested in. As a result the classroom is experienced by many children (particularly ADHD kids) as boring and unexciting. Students may have little investment in the educational process and are given little responsibility for their own education. Eventually, many creative and weirdly able children begin to despise both learning and school. This increases the stress on parents and families. Similar to MI theory, the student who is not invested in his education may be viewed as uncooperative and placed at risk for an ADHD label.

Problem-Posing Education

Freire (1970) proposes a new educational paradigm—problem-posing education. A problem-posing classroom is an exciting place and is never boring. Coexisting with the excitement is serious intellectual and academic engagement. Students are encouraged to challenge and question the teacher. The child's knowledge is respected and given equal weight to that of the teacher's. The problem-posing teacher values everyone's presence and pays particular attention to students who may be marginalized due to race, class, gender, sexual preference, or psychiatric label (ADHD, for example).

In this classroom environment all students are responsible for the educational process. Children have input on the curriculum and course content. The learning process becomes a collective effort between the teacher and the students. Dialogue, creativity, reflection, active participation, and critical thinking take place in such classrooms. It is a challenging approach but worthwhile in that children become awake in the class; they also learn to slow down and listen to others share their perspectives and opinions. In the sections to follow are ideas that help promote active learning.

Varying the Approach

The SMART teacher does not solely rely on the didactic lecture. Too much emphasis on the lecture reinforces the banking model and encourages passive learning behavior. Instead of getting right into the topic, it might be better to vary the teaching style and get the students more actively involved. To promote curiosity and dialogue, the teacher may propose a question, then place students in small groups to prompt participation.

SMART teacher Tracy Candini (personal communication, 1999) used critical pedagogy to bring forth his third graders' special talents. For instance, Tracy was noticing that eight-year-old Vincent was distracted during direct interaction time. Vincent always had his hands in his desk, playing with various objects. Frequently, his pencils became spaceships and erasers became giant asteroids traveling through space that would eventually end up on a direct collision course with each other. The audible explosions that occurred on impact not only interfered with Tracy's lecture but elicited inappropriate behaviors from the class.

Vincent could get so involved in his exploration that he did not hear verbal directions given to the whole class. If Tracy asked him to describe or repeat the directions, he frequently could not. Even when Tracy gave Vincent one-on-one time and clarified the directions, he had difficulty completing the tasks. Completing worksheets was not only ineffective for Vincent but also usually involved off-task and hyperactive behavior. Vincent was beginning to despise school. ADHD was in charge!

Tracy recognized that Vincent was a very creative child who had an extraordinary imagination. Vincent also had a lot to say, as he had verbal intelligence. To help engage him, Tracy developed a weekly assignment called Creativity. Creativity is an open-ended assignment Tracy gives to all students; the idea is to develop critical thinking skills and promote and harness their imagination. There are no wrong answers. A week's assignment might be to create a puppet, build a paper boat, or design a comic strip. But the assignment is more than just to create the project. The students must stand up in front of the class and talk about their creations.

Vincent loved the creativity assignments. He was free to use his imagination in a constructive way that allowed for self-expression. At the end of the week, Vincent's projects stood out as the most interesting. For Valentine's Day he made a mailbox with a moving hand that would retrieve his mail. His presentations were very informative and full of detail. Vincent's peers could hardly wait to see what inventions he would bring to school next.

By Tracy's varying his approach and using the Creativity technique, Vincent went from having a troublemaking reputation to being the student who was the most inventive and colorful in the class. His self-worth soared and he developed a new interest in school. ADHD still attempted to visit Vincent but didn't have the same hold on him.

Using Videos

Another way to promote engaged learning is to bring in a current video (or a movie or TV clip) that relates to a certain topic. For example, to promote a dialogue on getting along with other children, a SMART teacher could show a segment from an "Arthur" TV show (Brown, 1999) that highlights children resolving conflict. The teacher can then ask the students to discuss or role play the issue in pairs.

Finishing the Day with an Evaluative Exercise

At the end of the day, it might be helpful to ask the students to write down the most important thing they learned that day and the question foremost in their minds. Alternatively, students could be asked to use their "paying attention" power during a lecture. After the lecture they could be asked to summarize it. To promote students' involvement, the teacher could ask for feedback about how to improve the lecture.

Inviting Critical Feedback

To promote a democratic classroom, ongoing feedback from the students is crucial, especially from students with an ADHD diagnosis. Michael White (1995) states that so-called ADHD children are the most able critics of the educational process. Many are quite articulate at naming the irrelevance of traditional classroom structures and voicing the injustices of teasing and practices of exclusion. I have asked some ADHD children I have worked with for feedback on how to improve the educational system. Here is what they said:

- Use a lot of pictures (visual clues) to help me learn.
- Offer us choices.
- Be patient!
- Realize that I am intelligent.
- Don't just lecture—it's boring!
- Let me walk around the classroom.
- Know when to bend the rules.
- Don't give tons of homework.
- Notice when I am doing well.
- Don't tell the other kids that I am taking Ritalin.

- More recess!
- Recognize cultural and racial diversity.

Homeschooling

Homeschooling has become an increasingly popular educational alternative. A number of people homeschool for religious reasons. Others choose the homeschooling option because their child's learning style does not fit with the cookie-cutter approach of their local school. Many of these children are either ADHD or learning disabled.

Research shows that homeschooling works (Gallagher, 1999) for some kids who have unique and gifted learning styles—children who are bright and independent and learn naturally on their own. This is an option that I imagine Huck would have preferred. The freedom associated with homeschooling would have been appealing to Huck. He considered himself a boy of nature and had a natural curiosity. Learning in his own environment and at his own pace would have made school more exciting for him. He could have done science experiments on the Mississippi or history lessons on slavery with his friend, Jim (a runaway slave).

As stated earlier, many weirdly abled children find conventional school dull, and their intrinsic motivation dissipates. Homeschool can be the solution for some of these children. We (SMART therapists) discuss this as a legitimate option with families when their ADHD child is doing poorly in school. We often tell families that geniuses such as Thomas Edison were homeschooled. Offering homeschooling as a justifiable alternative fits with the SMART values of honoring difference, promoting diversity, and offering choices.

The largest barrier to homeschooling is the loss of income from a two-career household (Gallagher, 1999). Typically, one of the parents chooses to stay home to teach or guide the child. Yet some parents become quite resourceful and feel the benefits far outweigh the loss of income. Many parents tell me that staying home with their child improves their connection to them.

Another concern is the loss of socialization. It's been my experience that parents who homeschool find opportunities for their children to socialize, such as participating in athletics or dance. Most say it's not as big a problem as one may think. Children often tell me that they felt stuck with peers they didn't want to associate with (particularly bullies) when they were in school. Being homeschooled gives them the freedom to choose their friends and develop closer relationships.

We find that many children who have been put into the ADHD pigeonhole and who despise school resurrect their natural interest in learning once they are homeschooled. Often the child and the parent come up with creative teaching strategies that are missing in a large, assembly-line classroom. Often the ADHD label is rendered irrelevant once a child is out of the traditional school. Such was the case with Robert, diagnosed ADHD, and his family, who chose homeschooling after becoming frustrated with the limits and restraints of their local school.

Case Example: Robert Gets Homeschooled While Schooling ADHD

The following is a transcript of a conversation with Robert's mother, Jean, who supervised his homeschooling.

David: So does the description of ADHD fit Robert?

Jean: No way! He's just an active kid. He is just a different learner. He learns at his own pace. You need to be patient with him. He's a visual and auditory learner . . . both.

David: That's his personal learning style?

Jean: Yes.

David: And you're saying that his personal learning style didn't match up with the school's way of teaching . . . and thus, he was pathologized as ADHD?

Jean: Yes.

David: What do you think of that?

Jean: I think it's unfair. You shouldn't label kids like that. They began to think they can't accomplish much and it destroys their self-esteem.

David: Is that what happened to Robert?

Jean: Yes. His self-esteem was very low. Again, it's very unfair . . . he's just an active child.

David: How is it that you have been able to view Robert as an energetic kid and that he has these different learning preferences rather than seeing Robert as ADHD?

Jean: That came mostly when I started homeschooling Robert because I was able to observe him for long periods of time.

David: What did you learn when you observed him?

Jean: Well, I really watched his diet. No sugar! And I realized that he needed a break after thirty minutes. So after twenty minutes to a half-hour, he takes a study break and gets something to eat or goes to the restroom. And then he comes back and finishes the lesson.

David: And how did you come to that idea?

Jean: I learned on my own what to do with him. If I was going to be his best teacher, I needed to learn what kept him engaged as a learner, what motivated him . . . what his interests were. I had no teaching background so I learned as I went. I read a lot of math books. . . . I was bad at fractions!

David: What were some of the teaching strategies you developed that use Robert's learning style?

Jean: Well, in math we learned that you just can't give him a math worksheet with twenty questions and tell him to fill it out. I needed to explain the assignment and check with him every so often. With reading, we learned that Robert needs to read it out loud to retain it. He has to hear it out loud. I decided for us to act out characters in a play he was reading. I would play one character and he would play another. This way, he got really engaged and interested. At first, he didn't like it. But he saw how enthusiastic and energetic I was and he got into it! The more he read, the more he really got into it. The English book then had questions to answer about the play. He answered the questions so accurately . . . similar to the answers in the instructor's manual. I knew we had a breakthrough then—that he could really comprehend things by reading out loud.

David: Wow! So by experimentation you found ways that engaged him?

Jean: Yes, and now he enjoys learning and doesn't fight me about English or reading.

David: And how is he doing now?

Jean: I am very proud to say he made honor roll this semester! He got all B's.

David: What was that like for you?

Jean: I was ecstatic! I didn't think we could get to this point.

David: What did you learn about yourself in the process?

Jean: That with my conveying faith in him and me being motivated and creative, we could do it. And Robert is so proud. He never made honor roll before. Homework was a bad word for Robert. Now he likes it. He initiates his own work now. I don't have to remind him. Amazing!

David: What has this been like for you?

Jean: I can't tell you. He challenges himself. He's even talking about going to college. This is a kid who was labeled as lazy, a troublemaker, and ADHD.

David: What advice do you have for other parents and teachers?

Jean: Don't give up on your child. You need to find out what learning style your kid has and experiment. Once you find his particular way of learning, labels such as ADHD don't mean much. If more teachers tailored their teaching, fewer kids would be labeled. All kids are creative . . . you just have to be creative yourself to find it. I would also recommend home-schooling for some kids, like Robert, who don't fit in traditional schools. Kids who are different shouldn't be labeled.

David: Thanks Jean.

Thomas Edison once said, "Somewhere between the ages of eleven and fifteen, the average child begins to suffer from an atrophy, the paralysis of curiosity and the suspension of the power to observe. The trouble I should judge to lie with the schools" (Gallagher, 1999, p. 1). This chapter explores alternative teaching strategies that promote curiosity and reverse the troublesome trend of academic atrophy. SMART teaching accomplishes this by a unique blending of solution-focused class management, multiple intelligence theory, and critical pedagogy. These strategies promote hands-on learning, critical thinking, imagination, and active learning. If these strategies were used more often in the classroom, I believe that fewer students would be labeled ADHD. By privileging the unique learning styles of all children and focusing on their special talents, education becomes "the practice of freedom" (hooks, 1994, p. 9). I can imagine Huck Finn and other weirdly abled persons such as Thomas Edison calling on schools to offer children and families more of these educational alternatives, including homeschooling.

Chapter Eleven

Huck Gets Smart

A Conversation Between Huck and David

> Tom's most well, now, and got his bullet around his
> neck on a watch-guard for a watch, and is always
> seeing what time it is, and so there ain't nothing
> more to write about, and I am rotten glad of it,
> because if I'd a knowed what a trouble it was to
> make a book I wouldn't a tackled it and ain't
> agoing to no more. But I reckon I got to light out
> for the Territory ahead of the rest, because Aunt
> Sally she's going to adopt me and sivilize me and I
> can't stand it. I been there before.
> —*Huckleberry Finn in* The Adventures of Huckleberry Finn,
> *Mark Twain*

We've come to the end of our journey. Like Huck's odyssey down the Mississippi, we have explored territory beyond the bounds of "sivilization," challenging dominant notions about the ADHD diagnosis and its treatment. We have examined the effects of the pathologizing ADHD discourse on children, families, and clinicians and have uncovered a variety of therapeutic techniques that can help kids like Huck find their courage, abilities, and preferred futures.

Literary critics have praised Huckleberry Finn for his ingenuity, compassion, and higher moral values, taking note of his resistance to slavery and other dominant discourses of his time. Unfortunately, the critics also note that at the story's conclusion, Huck appears to be surrendering to yet another attempt to civilize him.

Under Tom's and his Aunt Sally's influence, Huck's commitment to his own preferred moral and social values begins to waver.

In this closing chapter, I'd like you to join Huck and me in an imaginary SMART interview. The interview occurs at the close of Mark Twain's novel, when Huck's Mississippi River journey ends. Let's see if we can build a life raft of support for Huck's courage and cultural resistance using the basic techniques of SMART therapy.

Huck and David's SMART Interview

Aunt Sally, custodial guardian of twelve-year-old Huckleberry Finn, seeks an ADHD assessment and treatment for Huckleberry, whom she seeks to adopt. She is concerned about Huckleberry because of his recent misconduct, including a flagrant disregard for rules, his running away, his refusal to go to school, as well as his lying, smoking, and attempting to free a slave while rafting on the Mississippi River. Let's turn to the interview.

David: Sally, what are your concerns?

Sally: It's Huck. He's really worrying me. For months, he's been traveling down the Mississippi River with a slave named Jim. We thought he was dead, for heaven's sake, and come to find out, he was just running around on a raft getting into all kinds of trouble . . . he's so defiant. He and my nephew, Tom, came up with a scheme to set Jim free and Tom ended up getting shot.

Huck: That wasn't my fault. If stupid Tom had told me Jim was already freed, we wouldn't have had to go through all that.

Sally: Well, Huck, that's just not the point.

David: These sound like big problems, Sally, and you seem quite concerned. Have you and Huck always had challenges like this?

Sally: Well, no—I can't say that. I just got Huck a while ago, the poor thing. His father was a complete drunk, ended up face down in the river. The boy lived with the Widow Douglas for a while, but Huck was just to wild for her. She tried to teach him right from wrong, tried to help him, even took him to see a psychiatrist—you may know him—Dr. Geigy? Well, they thought Huck might have ADHD, but the boy wouldn't have any of that. He flew the coop and went out on the river with Jim. I guess Huck's had these problems for a long time, David. I agree with Dr. Geigy—I think there's something wrong with this child's brain. Can you get him to take the medication we got for him?

David: Let me interview Huck first. Is that OK Sally?

Sally: Yes. Go right ahead.

David: Huck, is it OK if I ask you a few questions?

Huck: [Looking angry and uninterested] Oh, all right. . . . I've done this before.

David: What have you done before?

Huck: I met with Dr. Geigy . . . he tried to civilize me with Ritalin.

David: How did that affect you?

Huck: I didn't like it. I didn't want to be all drugged up. So I never took it. You're not going to make me take Ritalin are you?

David: Not if you and your family don't think it's helpful.

Huck: Good. So what do you want to ask me?

David: So, why do Aunt Sally and the Widow Douglas think you have ADHD?

Huck: I don't know. I guess 'cause I get all fidgety and stuff. And I don't take no stock in school either.

David: You don't like school?

Huck: No, all you do is read and write. It don't catch my fancy. But I did go to school most of the time I was living with the widow! I learned to spell and read and write just a little. I even could say my multiplication tables up to six times seven is thirty-five. I don't reckon I could get any further than that if I was to live forever!

David: You went to school most of the time? And you learned your times tables?

Huck: Yes.

David: Did ADHD or Trouble try to bother you in school?

Huck: I reckon a little. . . . I had a hard time sitting still and listening to the teacher 'bout stuff that I don't care nothing 'bout. I hated school at first, but by-and-by I got so I could stand it. The longer I went to school the easier it got to be.

David: As school got easier, what happened to ADHD?

Huck: It must have gone down river!

David: Wow! What does it say about you, Huck—that school got easier and ADHD went down river?

Huck: Oh shucks. I reckon I am smarter than I thought!

David: So why did you stop going to school and take a canoe down the Mississippi?

Huck: Because my Pap kidnaped me and beat me all the time. He even threatened to kill me. I had to run away. I even took a pig and axed his throat. I used the pig's blood to fake my own death.

David: So you ran away to save your life?

Huck: Yes.

David: And you came up with something quite ingenious by escaping your father! Would you have continued with school if Pap wasn't threatening you and beating you?

Huck: Yes, I reckon so.

David: Did you know this, Sally?

Sally: No, I didn't! Poor Huck. I'm so sorry.

David: What do you think it says about Huck in regards to how he escaped?

Sally: It says he is pretty darn shrewd!

David: Huck, do you think you are shrewder than Trouble and ADHD?

Huck: I guess so.

David: And what happened on the river, Huck? Did you like it?

Huck: I loved canoeing down the river. I felt free from civilization. It was on the shore that Trouble came!

David: I see. So I understand you met up with Jim. Is that true?

Huck: Why yes. He was Miss Watson's slave. Miss Watson was going to sell Jim off down river to slave owners. So Jim ran away. I met him down the river at Jackson Island. I was sort of lonely so it was nice to have such a good friend as Jim on the journey.

David: Would you consider Jim your friend, even though he is seen by your society as a slave?

Huck: Why yes. I mean I struggled and all but Jim was so dependable and trusting. He had such good sense. And Jim said that I was the best friend he ever had.

David: Why did Jim think you were such a good friend?

Huck: Well, I reckon 'cause I saved his life twice. Once on our journey two slave catchers were trying to catch Jim. I lied to them to protect him. Another time I was feeling guilty about helping Jim escape, so I wrote a letter to Miss Watson telling her where he was. Then I thought what Jim said—that I was his best friend. I said, all right then, I'll go to hell. And I tore up the letter.

David: Wow! Would it be OK if I saw your defiance to society as heroic?

Huck: What do you mean?

David: What I mean is that you listened to your own voice and stood up against racism. You stood for a higher moral purpose.

Huck: I never thought of it like that, but I guess you're right, David.

David: So if being civilized means supporting slavery and corruption, then perhaps being uncivilized is an act of courage and resistance.

Huck: I never thought of it like that. I thought I was sinning when I tore up that letter.

David: I would invite you to trust your own instincts and to be choosy about what you learn from society.

Huck: OK. I wish society could be like the river. On the river there was no slavery, just the freedom of the wilderness.

David: Would you say your free sprit is one of your best talents?

Huck: Yes.

David: What might happen if you trusted in your own instincts?

Huck: I might not have listened to Tom Sawyer's crazy ideas on how to free Jim. I should have listened to my own plan.

David: What do you mean?

Huck: Well, at the end of our journey, Jim was caught and put up as a prisoner in a hut behind Aunt Sally's house. I just wanted to steal the key and give it to Jim so he could head back down the river. Tom wanted to do this wild plan of digging a hole beneath the hut, sawing off the leg of the bed that Jim was chained to and then using a rope ladder and having Jim break out the window. This plan took three weeks! It was a miserable failure. A chase began and some men captured Jim when he escaped. Tom got shot by the men! He even wears the bullet he was shot with around his neck! It didn't need to happen. And then to find out Tom knew all along that Jim was already free. Tom told me that Miss Watson had died and freed Jim in her will!

David: So, what do you think of Tom's plotting—his schemes and deceits?

Huck: Well, I felt a little relieved that Tom was not a slave stealer. But I felt bad that Jim spent an extra three weeks as a slave when he was really a free person.

David: Can I ask a bit more about that?

Huck: Yes.

David: Where does the idea come from that slave stealing is bad?

Huck: I don't know . . . from society . . . church . . . adults . . . the slave catchers on the river . . .

David: And where does the idea come from that freeing Jim is a good thing?

Huck: Well, I guess that's my idea. I think all people should be free. It's hard to stick to my idea when everybody says it's bad.

David: If you listened to your own instincts—your own heart— what would you believe?

Huck: I believe in freedom!

David: Would it be fair to say that when society calls you a slave stealer, it's trying to steal your better judgment?

Huck: Yes.

David: Who seems to help you lose track of your better judgment?

Huck: Sometimes Tom . . .

David: Do you think that Trouble and ADHD get in the way of your judgment?

Huck: Trouble does, yes. I think Tom and Trouble are almost as good friends as me and Tom. But David, I don't think this ADHD thing really fits me.

David: What makes you say that?

Huck: Well, Dr. Geigy says kids that have ADHD are hyper and fidgety all the time and can't listen. But I had to listen a lot on the river. And I listened to Jim mighty close. And I did go to school. I've done lots of things that would surprise people.

David: Are you surprised, Sally?

Sally: Yes, I am.

David: Why are you surprised?

Sally: I didn't know that Huck learned a thing in school. And I thought he was messing around with Jim just to be rebellious. Now I see that Huck is a very moral and courageous person. And a very loving boy who stands up for what he believes.

David: So you are seeing Huck in a different light?

Sally: Why, yes.

David: Do you think Huck will stick with his good judgment and instincts. Or do you think Trouble and ADHD will recruit him back?

Sally: I imagine they will keep trying [laughs].

David: What do you now know about Huck that tells you he will succeed?

Sally: That he has a good mind and a wise heart. And as I hear more of this river adventure, he made good choices when Trouble could have taken over. But David, do you think these changes will continue at school?

David: I was just thinking about that. Do you think Huck's reputation as a troublemaker might dog him now that he's escaped a troubled lifestyle?

Sally: It might.

Huck: No, it won't! I wish others could hear this interview.

David: Do you think others need to be brought up to date with this newer version of you, Huck?

Huck: Yes, Judge Thatcher and my teacher—and Tom—and Dr. Geigy!

David: Perhaps we can write them a letter about your changes and your heroism?

Huck: Maybe you can do that. I don't take no stock in books. Writing the book about my journey was too much trouble!

David: OK, I will write it and get your approval and signature. Kind of like the collaboration you had with Jim on the Mississippi.

Huck: OK.

David: What do you want included in the letter?

Huck: That just because I like to smoke and take journeys on the river, it doesn't mean I am bad or ADHD—that I have a conscience and I am really trying to figure out how to follow the rules while listening to my own judgment.

David: Would it be fair to say that sometimes listening to your own conscience might mean rebelling against the rules of society?

Huck: Yes.

David: Do you think that other kids have similar struggles with following their own voice and the rules of society?

Huck: Yes. I think a lot do. I think a lot are tricked into thinking they are bad or have a disease like this ADHD thing . . . kids who like to smoke or like freedom . . . kids who are different.

David: And if you listen to your own conscience, what does it say about this ADHD thing?

Huck: I think it's a shame. Like some of the wild schemes and plots of Tom.

David: What do you mean?

Huck: Well, don't a lot a people profit from Ritalin and ADHD . . . like they profited from slavery?

David: I guess so.

Huck: Seems to me that kids know what's right and wrong . . . ADHD and Ritalin just get in the way.

David: Thanks Huck! Why don't we stop here? Do you think you need to reschedule at this time?

Huck: Nah. I'll give you a holler if I need something.

David: Is that OK, Sally?

Sally: Yes. Thanks, David!

David: Let's end here then OK?

Huck: OK.

Like Huckleberry Finn, who transcended the cultural dictates of his time, SMART therapy calls us to transcend the traditional approach to ADHD. It is a call to fight the increasing power of the pharmaceutical industry. It is a call to honor children's special and weird abilities. It is a call to honor difference rather than pathologize it. It is a challenge to let our creative consciences guide our profession rather than succumbing to the oppressive dictates of the Ritalin Nation. I hope you will join Huck and me as our journey of freedom continues. The future of our profession and of many children depends on it.

Reading List

The following are readings that provide information about working collaboratively and alternatively with ADHD children.

Armstrong, T. (1995). *The myth of the A.D.D. Child*. New York: Dutton.

Breeding, J. (1996). *The wildest colts make the best horses*. Austin, TX: Bright Books.

Breggin, P. (1998). *Talking back to Ritalin*. Monroe, ME: Common Courage Press.

DeGrandpre, R. *Ritalin nation: Rapid fire culture and the transformation of human consciousness*. New York: W. W. Norton.

Diller, L. (1998). *Running on Ritalin*. New York: Bantam Books.

Freeman, J. C., Epston, D., and Lobovits, D. (1997). *Playful approaches to serious problems: Narrative therapy with children and their families*. New York: W. W. Norton.

Hartmann, T. (1993). *Attention deficit disorder: A different perception*. Grass Valley, CA: Underwood Books.

Selekman, M. D. (1997). *Solution-focused therapy with children: Harnessing family strengths for systemic change*. New York: Guilford Press.

Smith, C., & Nylund, D. (Eds.). (1997). *Narrative therapies with children and adolescents*. New York: Guilford Press.

Stein, D. B. (1999). *Ritalin is not the answer: A drug-free, practical program for children diagnosed with ADD or ADHD*. San Francisco: Jossey-Bass.

Zimmerman, J. L., and Dickerson, V. C. (1996). *If problems talked: Narrative therapy in action*. New York: Guilford Press.

The following are websites that offer alternative views on ADHD:

www.borntoexplore.org

www.narrativeapproaches.com

www.treating huck.com

References

ADHD: Not a myth! (1996, September). *CHADD Newsletter*, p. 1.

American Psychiatric Association. (1994). *Diagnostic and statistical manual of mental disorders* (4th ed.). Washington, DC: Author.

Andersen, T. (Ed.). (1991). *The reflecting team: Dialogues and dialogues about the dialogues*. New York: W. W. Norton.

Anderson, H. (1997). *Conversation, language, and possibilities: A postmodern approach to psychotherapy*. New York: Guilford Press.

Anderson, H., & Goolishian, H. (1988). Human systems as linguistic systems: Preliminary and evolving ideas about the implications for clinical theory. *Family Process, 27*, 371–393.

Anderson, H., & Goolishian, H. (1992). The client is the expert: A not-knowing approach to therapy. In S. McNamee & K. J. Gergen (Eds.), *Therapy as social construction* (pp. 25–39). Thousand Oaks, CA: Sage.

Armstrong, T. (1995). *The myth of the A.D.D. child*. New York: Dutton.

Barkley, R. A. (1990). *Attention deficit hyperactivity disorder: A handbook for diagnosis and treatment*. New York: Guilford Press.

Bateson, G. (1972). *Steps to an ecology of mind*. New York: Ballantine.

Berg, I. K. (1994). *Family based services: A solution-focused approach*. New York: W. W. Norton.

Berg, I. K., & Miller, S. D. (1992). *Working with the problem drinker: A solution-focused approach*. New York: W. W. Norton.

Biederman, J., & others. (1995). Family-environment risk factors for attention deficit hyperactivity disorder. *Archives of General Psychiatry, 52*, 464–470.

Breeding, J. (1996). *The wildest colts make the best horses*. Austin, TX: Bright Books.

Breggin, P. (1998). *Talking back to Ritalin*. Monroe, ME: Common Courage Press.

Brown, M. (1999). Arthur Television Series on PBS.

Bruner, J. (1986). *Acts of meaning*. Cambridge, MA: Harvard University Press.

Buchanan, B., & Stayton, C. (1994). *The hype about hyperactivity*. Paper presented at the 17th Annual Family Therapy Networker Symposium, Chicago.

Cade, B. (1990). The mini-tornado: Turning hyperactivity into energy. *Family Therapy Case Studies, 5*(1), 45–50.

Caplan, P. (1995). *They say you're crazy: How the world's most powerful psychiatrists decide who's normal.* New York: Addison-Wesley.

Chang, J. (1998). Children's stories, children's solutions: Social constructionist therapy for children and their families. In M. F. Hoyt (Ed.), *The handbook of constructive therapies* (pp. 251–275). San Francisco: Jossey-Bass.

Connors, K. (1989). *Conners parents' rating scale-revised and Conners teachers' rating scale-revised.* North Towanda, NY: Multi-Health Systems.

Cramond, D. The coincidence of attention deficit hyperactivity disorder and creativity. *The National Research Center on the Gifted and Talented, 1*(1), 1–17.

Cushman, P. (1995). *Constructing the self, constructing America.* New York: Addison-Wesley.

DeGrandpre, R. (1999). *Ritalin nation: Rapid fire culture and the transformation of human consciousness.* New York: W. W. Norton.

Derrida, J. (1981). *Positions.* Chicago: University of Chicago Press.

de Shazer, S. (1985). *Keys to solutions in brief therapy.* New York: W. W. Norton.

de Shazer, S. (1988). *Clues: Investigating solutions in brief therapy.* New York: W. W. Norton.

de Shazer, S. (1991). *Putting difference to work.* New York: W. W. Norton.

de Shazer, S. (1994). *Words were originally magic.* New York: W. W. Norton.

Diller, L. (1998). *Running on Ritalin.* New York: Bantam Books.

Epston, D. (1993). Internalizing discourses versus internalizing discourses. In S. Gilligan & R. Price (Eds.), *Therapeutic conversations* (pp. 161–180). New York: Guilford Press.

Epston, D. (1994). Extending the conversation. *Family Therapy Networker, 18,* 31–37, 62–63.

Epston, D. (1997). A chronicle of therapy: Annals of the "new Dave." *Gecko, 3,* 59–85.

Epston, D., & White, M. (1990). "Consulting your consultants: The documentation of alternative knowledges." *Dulwich Centre Newsletter, 4,* 25–35.

Foucault, M. (1973). *The birth of the clinic.* London: Tavistock.

Freedman, J. L., & Combs, G. (1996). *Narrative therapy: The social construction of preferred realities.* New York: W. W. Norton.

Freeman, J. C., Epston, D., & Lobovits, D. (1997). *Playful approaches to serious problems: Narrative therapy with children and their families.* New York: W. W. Norton.

Freire, P. (1970). *Pedagogy of the oppressed.* New York: Continuum.

Furman, B., & Ahola, T. (1992). *Solution talk: Hosting therapeutic conversations.* New York: W. W. Norton.

Gallagher, T. (1999). Born to explore: The other side of ADD. [http: www. borntoexplore.com].

Gardner, H. (1983). *Frames of mind.* New York: Basic Books.

Giroux, H. A. (1992). *Border crossing: Cultural workers and the politics of education.* New York: Routledge.

Golden, G. S. (1991). Role of attention deficit hyperactivity disorder in learning disabilities. *Seminars in Neurology, 11*, 35–41.

Griffith, J. L., & Griffith, M. E. (1994). *The body speaks: Therapeutic dialogues for mind-body problems*. New York: Basic Books.

Hallowell, E. M., and Ratey, J. J. (1994). *Driven to distraction*. New York: Pantheon.

hooks, b. (1994). *Teaching to transgress: Education as the practice of freedom*. New York: Routledge.

Hubble, M., & O'Hanlon, W. H. (1992). Theory countertransference. *Dulwich Centre Newsletter, 1*, 25–30.

Hyans, J. (1979). *Zen in the martial arts*. New York: Bantam Books.

Kirk, S., & Kutchins, H. (1992). *The selling of DSM: The rhetoric of science in psychiatry*. New York: Aldine DeGruyter.

Law, I. (1997). Attention deficit disorder: Therapy with a shoddily built construct. In C. Smith & D. Nylund (Eds.), *Narrative therapies with children and adolescents* (pp. 282–306). New York: Guilford Press.

Madigan, S. P. (1996). The politics of identity: Considering community discourse in the externalizing of internalized problem discourses. *Journal of Systemic Therapies, 15*(1), 47–62.

Madigan, S. P. (1997). "Reconsidering memory: Re-membering lost identities back towards re-membered selves." In C. Smith & D. Nylund (Eds.), *Narrative therapies with children and adolescents* (pp. 336–355). New York: Oxford Press.

Madigan, S. P., & Epston, D. (1995). From "spy-chiatric gaze" to communities of concern: From monologue to dialogue. In S. Friedman (Ed.), *The reflecting team in action: Collaborative practice in family therapy* (pp. 257–276). New York: Guilford Press.

Metcalf, L. (1997). *Parenting towards solutions*. West Nyack, NY: The Center for Applied Research in Education.

Metcalf, L. (1999). *Teaching towards solutions*. West Nyack, NY: The Center for Applied Research in Education.

Miller, S. D., Hubble, M. A., and Duncan, B. L. (Eds.). (1996). *The handbook of solution-focused brief therapy*. San Francisco: Jossey-Bass.

Monk, G., Winslade, J., Crocket, K., and Epston, D. (Eds.). (1997). *Narrative therapy in practice: The archeology of hope*. San Francisco: Jossey-Bass.

Nichols, M. P., and Schwartz, R. C. (Eds.). (1995). *Family therapy: Concepts and methods*. Boston: Allyn & Bacon.

Nylund, D., & Corsiglia, V. (1994). Attention to the deficits in attention deficit disorder: Deconstructing the diagnosis and bringing forth children's special abilities. *Journal of Collaborative Therapies, 2*, 7–17.

Nylund, D., and Corsiglia, V. (1996). From deficits to special abilities: Working narratively with children labeled ADHD. In M. Hoyt (Ed.), *Constructive therapies 2* (pp. 163–183). New York: Guilford Press.

Nylund, D., & Thomas J. (1994). The economics of narrative. *Family Therapy Networker, 18,* 38–39.

O' Hanlon, W. H., & Weiner-Davis, M. (1989). *In search of solutions: A new direction in psychotherapy.* New York: W. W. Norton.

Osenton, T., & Chang, J. (1999). Solution-oriented classroom management: Application with young children. *Journal of Systemic Therapies, 18*(2), 65–76.

Parry, A., & Doan, R. E. (1994). *Story re-visions: Narrative therapy in the postmodern world.* New York: Guilford Press.

Rapoport, J. L., & others. (1978). Dextroamphetamine: Cognitive and behavioral effects in normal and hyperactive boys and men. *Archives General Psychiatry, 37,* 933–943.

Reid, R., & others. (1994). An analysis of teachers' perceptions of attention deficit hyperactivity disorder. *Journal of Research and Development in Education, 27,* 745–753.

Roth, S., & Epston, D. (1996). Consulting the problem about the problematic relationship: An exercise for experiencing a relationship with an externalized problem. In M. F. Hoyt (Eds.), *Constructive Therapies 2* (pp. 148–162). New York: Guilford Press.

Selekman, M. D. (1997). *Solution-focused therapy with children: Harnessing family strengths for systemic change.* New York: Guilford Press.

Shor, I. (1992). *Empowering education: Critical teaching for social change.* Chicago: University of Chicago Press.

Smith, C. (1997). Introduction: Comparing traditional therapies with narrative approaches. In C. Smith & D. Nylund (Eds.), *Narrative therapies with children and adolescents* (pp. 1–52). New York: Guilford Press.

Smith, C., & Nylund, D. (Eds.). (1997). *Narrative therapies with children and adolescents.* New York: Guilford Press.

Stewart, B., & Nodrick, B. (1990). The learning disability lifestyle: From reification to liberation. *Family Therapy Case Studies, 5*(1), 61–73.

Twain, M. (1999). *Adventures of Huckleberry Finn.* New York: Oxford University Press. (Original work published 1884)

Turner, V., & Bruner, E. (Eds.). (1986). *The anthropology of experience.* Chicago: University of Illinois Press.

van Gennep, A. (1960). *The rites of passage.* Chicago: University of Chicago Press.

Walter, J. L., and Peller, J. E. (1992). Become solution-focused in brief therapy. New York: Brunner/Mazel.

White, M. (1989, Summer). The externalizing of the problem and the reauthoring of lives and relationships. *Dulwich Centre Newsletter,* pp. 3–20.

White, M. (1991). Deconstruction and therapy. *Dulwich Centre Newsletter, 3,* 1–21.

White, M. (1995). Schools as communities of acknowledgment. *Dulwich Centre Newsletter, 2 & 3*, 51–66.

White, M., & Epston, D. (1990). *Narrative means to therapeutic ends*. New York: W. W. Norton.

Winslade, J., & Monk, G. (1999). *Narrative counseling in schools: Powerful and brief*. Thousand Oaks, CA: Corwin Press.

Wolraich, M. L., & others. (1996). Comparison of diagnostic criteria for attention deficit hyperactivity disorder in a countrywide sample. *Journal of the American Academy of Child and Adolescent Psychiatry, 34*, 319–324.

Zametkin, A. J., & others. (1990). Cerebral glucose metabolism in adults with hyperactivity of child onset. *New England Journal of Medicine, 323*, 1361–1366.

Zametkin, A. J., & others. (1993). Brain metabolism in teenagers with attention deficit hyperactivity disorder. *Archives of General Psychiatry, 50*, 333–340.

Zimmerman, J. L., & Dickerson, V. C. (1996). *If problems talked: Narrative therapy in action*. New York: Guilford Press.

Index

The Author

David Nylund is a licensed clinical social worker at Kaiser Permanente in Stockton, California, where he serves as the coordinator of training. In addition, he is a clinical supervisor at La Familia Counseling Center in Sacramento, California. He is also on the adjunct faculty at both the Professional School of Psychology and the Division of Social Work at California State University, Sacramento.

Nylund has authored or coauthored several articles on narrative therapy in journals such as *The Family Therapy Networker*, the *Dulwich Centre Newsletter*, and the *Journal of Systemic Therapies*. He has cowritten chapters in *Constructive Therapies 2* and the *Handbook of Constructive Therapies*. He and Craig Smith coedited *Narrative Therapies with Children and Adolescents*. He also serves as a consulting editor to the journal, *Social Work*.

In addition to his writing, Nylund conducts national training workshops on narrative therapy. His current interests are poststructuralist theory, cultural studies, gender studies, masculinities, child and family therapy, and critical pedagogy.

David lives with his partner, Debora, and his son, Drake, in Sacramento, California. You can log on to his website at www.treatinghuck.com.